W9-ALJ-527

Isola Asinara

Golfo
dell'Asinara

Olbia

Porto Torres

Berchidda

Sassari

Lago del Coghinas

Alghero

Orosei

Nuoro

Golfo di
Orosei

Lago Omodeo

Oristano

Arbatax

Golfo di
Oristano

Iglesias

Isola di
San Pietro

Carbonia

Cagliari

Carloforte

Golfo di
Cagliari

Isola di
Sant'Antioco

SARDINIA

The Mediterranean Flavors of Sardinia

Sweet Myrtle

Efisio Farris
with Jim Eber

Food Photography by Laurie Smith
Location Photography by Rohan Van Twest

RIZZOLI
NEW YORK

& Bitter Honey

First published in the United States of America in 2007
by Rizzoli International Publications, Inc.
300 Park Avenue South
New York, NY 10010
www.rizzoliusa.com

© 2007 GourmetSardinia Co.

Food photographs © Laurie Smith (pages 1, 28, 38, 43, 49, 65, 66, 69, 73,
77, 83, 88, 89, 90, 97, 99, 100, 107, 108, 117, 118, 121, 137, 143, 144, 151,
159, 163, 165, 169, 187, 205, 206, 211, 215, 219, 220, 223, 227, 247)
Food photography styling by Erica McNeish
Archival photographs © Efisio Farris (pages 11, 15, 37, 40, 41, 47, 53, 57,
72, 129, 130 (bottom), 131, 135, 149, 161, 162, 167, 183, 221, 250, 253)
All other photographs © Rohan Van Twest

All rights reserved. No part of this publication may be reproduced, stored in a retrieval system,
or transmitted in any form or by any means, electronic, mechanical, photocopying, recording, or
otherwise, without prior consent of the publishers.

2007 2008 2009 2010 / 10 9 8 7 6 5 4 3 2 1

Distributed in the U.S. trade by Random House, New York

Printed in China

Designed by Laura Lindgren

ISBN-10: 0-8478-2992-8
ISBN-13: 978-0-8478-2992-7

Library of Congress Catalog Control Number: 2007925274

To the women who inspire me—
my grandmothers, my mother, my aunts, my sisters,
and especially my wife and daughter

Contents

Pastas & Risottos

Main Courses

Desserts

◇　◇　◇

Sa cuchina minore no timet su fuste.

◆

"Simple cuisine makes the home great."

Welcome

My father never knew a stranger. When he met people, he invited them to come inside. And eat. He'd introduce my mother and then bring out a tray carrying a few small glasses, which he'd fill with his own wine. Together, everyone would raise a glass, look each other in the eye, and offer a simple toast: *Salute*. My mother would then bring out a little food–some sausage, cheese, a few olives–and they would begin to talk: politics, family, how to graft an olive tree. For my father, food started the conversation; he knew the best way to get to know someone was around the table. For my mother, food was love.

Despite the suspicious expressions of men talking in the town square, of the women sweeping up in front of their homes, and of the shepherds and fishermen working the land and sea, Sardinians are the most hospitable people on Earth. In Sardinia, hospitality is sacred. It is an essential part of our history and identity. We are raised to be gracious and gregarious. We just don't want to get to know you too quickly. You cannot simply go to Sardinia and expect to hear all of our stories, recipes, ingredients, and secrets. You need to be invited inside and linger–to join us at the table and talk. And eat.

D. H. Lawrence ran into this "Sardinian paradox" when he journeyed from his home in Sicily to tour Sardinia for nine days. While stunned by the beauty of the island, finding great joy in our sky, sea, and stones, he was equally stunned by Sardinia's distance and difference from mainland Italy–the island's seemingly poor conditions and its people who "won't give you a crust of bread." But with all due respect to his beautifully written *Sea and Sardinia*, D. H. Lawrence came–and left–a stranger.

I am not a stranger; this is my home. *Salute*. Welcome to the table.

History Matters

From the moment you sit down at our table, the important thing is not how much we serve you but that we welcome you by serving the best of what we have. In my family that usually meant some pane carasau (Sardinian music bread), pecorino, sausage, and my father's olives or baby artichokes preserved in oil, perhaps then a plate of pasta or a dish from the "cucina rustica."

It is also important that we serve some of what we have made or grown ourselves; Sardinian cuisine relies on fresh ingredients and straightforward preparations to preserve and enhance the flavor of those ingredients. The foundation is simple and rustic, uncomplicated yet hearty, deep in flavor and texture–not to mention tradition (many recipes have changed little over centuries and are tied to ancient customs and habits) and variety (only Sicily and Piedmont rival our agricultural production).

Meat, cheese, and pasta are the most prominent staples of our diet. Though seafood is now very popular, most fish dishes, aside from a few, date back no more than a couple of centuries–young by Sardinian standards. Despite 1,800 kilometers of magnificent coastline–pure white sands, hidden coves and grottos, picturesque cliffs that soar above caves and rocks framed by the bluest sea and sky–Sardinia does not have an ancient seafaring tradition. We are known as a "nation of shepherds": more than one hundred thousand shepherds live in Sardinia, and sheep outnumber people on the island three to one. Moreover, our most populated regions and deepest cultural and culinary traditions tend to be inland.

THE SIZE OF SARDINIA

Sardinia is the second largest island in the Mediterranean—a little smaller than Sicily. But Sardinia is also the fourth least populated region in Italy, with well under two million inhabitants. With about 200 kilometers between us and the Italian mainland, we consider our island a nation state and many of us still refer to Italy as "the continent."

Why inland? One word: raids. The Phoenicians came first in 880 BC, followed by Carthaginians, Romans, Vandals, Byzantines, Arabs, Spanish, and a few others, until we became part of Italy in the 1850s. We've maintained our fiery spirit and good humor through it all, but for thousands of years we believed the sea brought nothing but trouble.

Thus, although the island is Italian, only a small part of the character of our food reflects the mainland. Some of the pasta shapes, meats and cheeses (like lamb and pecorino), and, of course, olive oil will be familiar. But lingering Roman, Arabian, Moorish, Catalan, and other Mediterranean influences (like myrtle and saffron) make our cuisine a hybrid that also includes many indigenous Sardinian ingredients, wines, liquors, and cheeses. All of these ingredients–some harder to find than others–are explained in recipes and sidebars throughout the book, and the pantry section in the back can help locate them. Yet no single cookbook can hope to capture it all, and I did not even pretend to try. Think of this book as a journey to my family's table. I promise you will come away with an intimate knowledge of this remarkable island.

OROSEI

"Oh wonderful Orosei, with your almonds and your reedy river, throbbing, throbbing with light and the sea's nearness, and all so lost, in a world gone by, lingering as legends linger on. It is hard to believe it is real."

—D. H. Lawrence, *The Sea and Sardinia* (1921)

Lawrence's words painted a perfect picture of my hometown. Orosei is a small beachside town on the eastern coast of the island between Mount Tuttavista and the Cedrino River. With shepherds tending pastures and fishermen trolling the sea, hills filled with wild produce and cultivated gardens and farms, vineyards of olives and grapes and a river once packed with trout and eel, Orosei embraces ingredients from land and sea. Historically, Orosei has seen times of great wealth and importance and survived much harder times. The medieval town center has basalt and stone homes dating from the fifteenth century, while more modern buildings have been built near the sea. Meadows, hills, and mountains frame the brilliant blues and greens of the water and spectacular beaches of white sand with rocky stretches perfect for hunting shellfish to the north. In this book, my family, our stories, and Orosei will serve as the foundation for the recipes as well as for understanding the history and flavors of the island.

ABOUT MY FAMILY AND MY NAME

My family has called Orosei home for centuries, and all the "characters" in the story of this book—my father and mother (Giuliano and Caterina), my sisters and brothers, my grandparents, and most of my aunts and uncles—were born there. In telling our stories, I have chosen to refer to them as I do in life: Mannoi and Mannai for grandfather and grandmother (like Mannoi Arre and Mannai Carta) and Zio and Zia for uncle and aunt (like Zio Pietro and Zia Maria).

I am named after the patron saint of Sardinia, Sant'Efisio (St. Efisio). St. Efisio was a Roman soldier who converted to Christianity in the third century. In 303 AD, Sardinian barbarians beheaded him at Nora for refusing to give up his religion. On May 1, the Festival of St. Efisio takes place in Cagliari, the capital of Sardinia, and is attended by pilgrims and spectators from all over the island. For more than 350 years, since an outbreak of plague in Cagliari, islanders have believed this festival in St. Efisio's honor protects them against pestilence. Drummers and musicians playing ancient instruments lead a magnificent procession of men and women in traditional Sardinian dress. Following them is a cart, pulled by a pair of *voes ruios* ("red cows," see page 172) and carrying St. Efisio's image from the capital to the church at Pula and then on to Nora the next day. Finally, we celebrate (as we do at most festivals) with a glorious feast.

Starters

Intradas

◈

Chie bene comintzat . . . bene finet.

"Who begins well, ends well."

Intradas are the most personal part of the Sardinian table, but what you would probably call appetizers–soups, salads, hot and cold smaller dishes–have never been a significant part of everyday meals in Sardinia. They often *were* everyday meals. The intradas I chose for this book are not the Italian-style antipasti you now find on the island, but recipes that will introduce you to some of the vibrant, diverse flavors and textures of Sardinian cuisine and which feature our most ancient indigenous ingredients, like bottarga and pane carasau. Some are from the sea, some from the land, and some from both. Many are from my family. Some come from local fisherman, farmers, and shepherds. And a few reflect more modern Sardinian combinations using our most traditional ingredients. But all of the intradas are designed to do one thing: welcome your family, friends, and guests to the table.

Breaking Bread

In Sardinia, bread is synonymous with life: when we think of food, we think of bread. In tough times, one piece of bread can be everything, and if you had just a little, you had a lot. In the fields, the space reserved for grain has always been bigger than that for other important ingredients like olives and grapes. The island was a *granaio* for the Romans and Phoenicians–a principal source of grain for their empires. Bread is such an essential part of our table and culture that we say about someone of exceptionally good character *vonu comente su pane* ("good like the bread").

Knowing this, it should come as no surprise that Sardinians are master bakers and that the first recipe in this book is for bread. But it is also the only bread recipe. This is because every region, down to each village, has had its own bread styles, sizes, techniques, and recipes for centuries. Adding to the variety, until wheat flour was available across the island, Sardinians made bread from whatever we had access to (such as acorns). Even today, there are hundreds, perhaps thousands, of bread variations. Moreover, commercial baking is a relatively new concept in Sardinia. In Orosei, there were (and still are) only two professional bakers that sold bread and other baked goods.

Most baking ovens were in homes, which is why the breads I know most about are

those made in my family. Simply put, baking bread is very personal for us and reflects intimate, almost sacred traditions. In my family, Zia Mary and Zia Zizzi were the bakers, and the most important baking days were the monthly daylong rituals of baking pane carasau, a thin flatbread baked to an absolute crisp to give it a long shelf life.

Pane carasau is the bread of the shepherds, who carried it on their long journeys to the mountains. They ate it with a little sheep's milk cheese, olive oil, or by itself. Sometimes referred to as *carta da musica* or "music bread" (for its resemblance to the thin parchment once used for sacred music scores), it is also extremely versatile and can be broken to use as an eating utensil or wetted to impart a noodlelike consistency. Though most common in the shepherd areas, especially the mountains surrounding Nuoro, pane carasau has become one of our most impressive traditions and can be found almost anywhere in Sardinia.

Baking pane carasau, like all of baking day, has a precise sequence, and my aunts instilled in me a reverence and respect for every part. (Only touch the dough with clean hands and never waste bread–any scraps not eaten can be shared with the animals and come back to us in another way.) Using a long wooden spatula, they fed the dough into a very hot oven until it puffed like a bubble (called *pane lentu*), which was then removed, split in half, stacked, and covered with linen cloths called *pannos de linu* to keep warm. After all the dough is made into pane lentu, the halves are then toasted to make pane carasau (*carasau* means "toasted" in Sardo, see page 22).

This recipe follows a similar sequence to my aunts' but produces far less than my family's monthlong supply. Today,

almost all Sardinians buy their pane carasau instead of spending an entire day making it. As a result, bakers like my friend Andrea and his family in Irgoli spend almost every day of the month making it. In busy times, they work for thirteen hours a day to make more than 1,400 pounds of pane carasau. But although the bakery uses a commercial oven and a few modern conveniences, they still do most of the work by hand, just as my aunts did years ago.

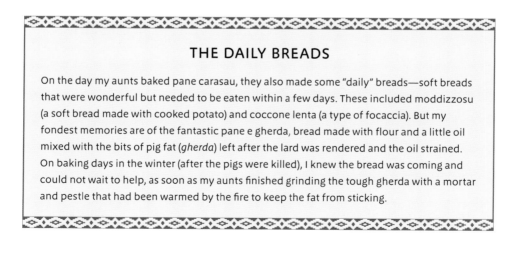

THE DAILY BREADS

On the day my aunts baked pane carasau, they also made some "daily" breads—soft breads that were wonderful but needed to be eaten within a few days. These included moddizzosu (a soft bread made with cooked potato) and coccone lenta (a type of focaccia). But my fondest memories are of the fantastic pane e gherda, bread made with flour and a little oil mixed with the bits of pig fat (*gherda*) left after the lard was rendered and the oil strained. On baking days in the winter (after the pigs were killed), I knew the bread was coming and could not wait to help, as soon as my aunts finished grinding the tough gherda with a mortar and pestle that had been warmed by the fire to keep the fat from sticking.

Sardinian music bread
Pane Carasau

MAKES ABOUT 30 SHEETS

On a work surface, thoroughly mix both types of flour. Form into a mound, making a well in the center. Dissolve the yeast in a small amount of warm water and let it sit until it begins to bubble. Stir the salt into 3 to 4 cups of warm water. Gradually incorporate yeast mixture and salted water into the well, using only as much of the salted water as you need to form a dough. Continue to mix until a firm dough is formed. Knead the dough until smooth and form it into a ball.

8 cups all-purpose flour, plus more for dusting
7¼ cups durum flour
3 envelopes active dry yeast
¾ teaspoon salt

Cut the dough into about 15 even pieces, each about the size of a fist. Roll each piece into a small ball using your hands, cupping your hands around each piece to give it a nicely taut shape. Flatten each ball by hand, then use a rolling pin to flatten each disk into a round sheet 12 to 14 inches in diameter.

Lightly flour several large kitchen towels. Layer the round sheets in the towels, sprinkling flour on each to prevent sticking. Let rest at room temperature for 2 hours.

Place a large baking stone on the center oven rack and preheat the oven and stone to 500°F.

Slide each dough sheet onto the hot baking stone in the preheated oven and bake until the bread begins to rise (about 30 seconds). Flip the bread and bake until it rises completely (about 30 seconds).

Remove the puffed bread from the oven and split into two sheets. Stack cut sheets aside covered with a cloth and weighted with a baking sheet. Continue baking and splitting the flattened disks of dough one by one until all are cooked.

Reduce heat to 325°F. Return the bread to the oven until toasted (2 to 3 minutes), moving frequently to prevent burning. Stack toasted pane carasau in linen and top with a weight until cool to prevent curling.

PANE GUTTIAU

My father says you need three things to cook anything: fire, olive oil, and salt. Pane guttiau is a perfect example. When pane carasau is drizzled with extra virgin olive oil, sprinkled with fine sea salt, and toasted golden brown, it is called pane guttiau. *Guttiau* means "sprinkle like raindrops" in Sardinian, which is what you do with the olive oil and sea salt. Simply drizzle each piece of pane carasau with a tablespoon of extra virgin olive oil and sprinkle with a pinch of sea or kosher salt before toasting in a 450 degree oven or grill until golden brown. For a twist on traditional garlic bread, mix a few smashed cloves of garlic into the oil before drizzling.

PANNOS DE LINU

When I was growing up, Sardinian homes were, like the island itself, almost completely self-sufficient. We had an oven to bake the bread, a cantina to store dry goods, a garden, a courtyard with animals, and a cart to take to the fields to harvest the grapes, olives, vegetables, and grain we needed to survive. Every home also had a loom called a *telaio*, which we used to make all our linens including the pannos de linu: a linen cloth that is essential to and made expressly for the monthly baking of pane carasau. It is first used to cover the dough as it rises and is then folded with the sheets of dough as they are rolled out. When the baked bread is split, the halves are stacked and covered with the pannos de linu to keep warm and again after they have been toasted into pane carasau. Finally, the bread is wrapped in the pannos de linu to take home, after which the cloth is rolled up like a carpet to store until the next baking day.

Bruschetta trio
Assazos de Brusketta

In Orosei, spring arrives when the shepherds bring the lambs; the fields overflow with artichokes, fennel, asparagus, and dandelion next to brilliant carpets of wildflowers and trees full with almond blossoms. Summer announces itself with figs and peaches and watermelon and the freshest seafood. The figs return to start the fall along with walnuts, almonds, and chestnuts. As they fade, in November and December, it is the beginning of the end. The grapes are harvested for wine and the olives for oil. Winter truly begins with the "ends" of the pigs; our shelves are stocked with potatoes and jars of tomatoes and vegetables, and we wait for the next season cycle.

I decided on this bruschetta trio to welcome you to the table. Together, they feature a good selection of Sardinian flavors and ingredients: pecorino, bitter honey, and abbamele (see pages 229 and 59)—a good beginning indeed.

Bruschetta with salsicce and pecorino
Brusketta a Sa Sarda
SERVES 4

Toast bread slices in oven or on a grill.

Top toasted bread slices with sausage and crumbles of the pecorino. Finish with a drizzling of olive oil.

4 slices paesano bread (¼-inch thick, hard-crusted)

12 slices dry aged sausage (or salami)

1 ounce Pecorino Sardo stagionato cheese (or other semi-aged pecorino cheese), crumbled

1 to 2 tablespoons extra virgin olive oil

Bruschetta with oyster mushrooms, ricotta, and bitter honey
Brusketta kin Cardula
SERVES 4

Toast bread slices in oven or on a grill.

Heat olive oil in a medium saucepan over medium heat, add garlic stirring until browned. Add mushrooms and parsley and sauté for 5 minutes. Season with salt and pepper to taste. Spoon the mushroom mixture onto the toasted bread. Top with a spoonful of the fresh ricotta and then drizzle with the bitter honey. Finish with freshly ground black pepper.

4 slices paesano bread (¼-inch thick, hard-crusted)
1 tablespoon extra virgin olive oil
1 garlic clove, minced
¼ pound oyster mushrooms, coarsely chopped
½ bunch flat leaf parsley, chopped
Sea salt and freshly ground black pepper
¼ cup sheep's milk ricotta cheese (or other creamy ricotta cheese)
1 tablespoon bitter honey (see page 229)

Bruschetta with chicory, goat cheese, and abbamele
Brusketta kin Zicoria
SERVES 4

Toast bread slices in oven or on a grill.

Wash the chicory thoroughly and chop in to 1½-inch pieces. Heat the olive oil in a medium skillet over medium heat. Add the halved garlic and mash in the skillet to release oils. Sauté until browned. Remove garlic and discard. Add chicory and sauté until tender (about 5 minutes). Season with salt and pepper to taste. Top toasted bread with the chicory and a spoonful of goat cheese. Finish with a drizzling of abbamele.

4 slices paesano bread (¼-inch thick, hard-crusted)
¼ pound chicory or red dandelion leaves
1 tablespoon extra virgin olive oil
1 garlic clove, halved
Sea salt and freshly ground black pepper
2 tablespoons goat cheese
1 tablespoon abbamele (see page 59)

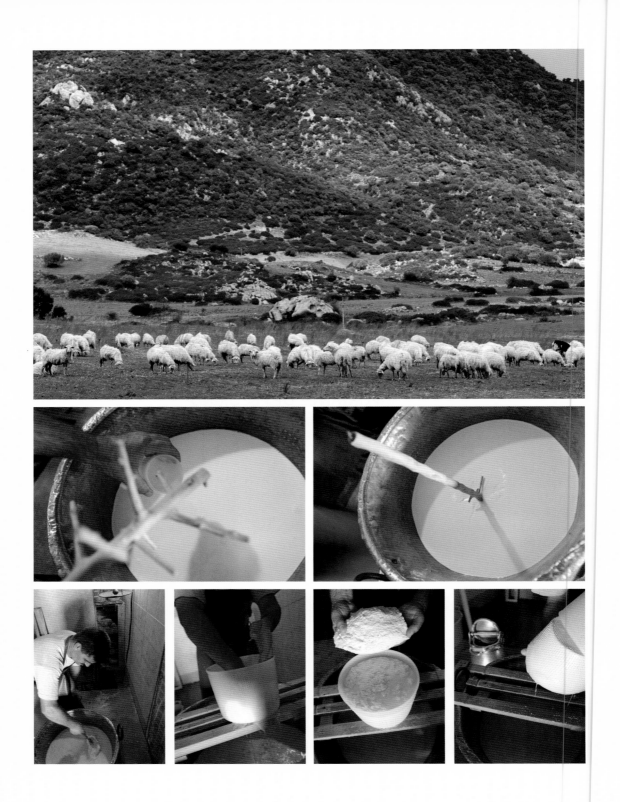

THE IMPORTANCE OF PECORINO

Pecorino is cheese made from sheep's milk, and the variations of pecorinos in Sardinia are dizzying. The flavor of the cheese can differ subtly and strongly from region to region, as can the aging process: fresh or young (aged up to two months and first made in late winter when the ewes are full with milk just after birthing time), semi-stagionato (aged from three to six months), and stagionato (aged up to twelve months). Two varieties, Pecorino Sardo and Fiore Sardo are DOP (Denominazióne di Origine Protetta); they come only from Sardinia. If you think you have never tasted pecorino from Sardinia, think again: the vast majority of Pecorino Romano (DOP) is produced on the island.

The economic importance of pecorino to Sardinia cannot be understated, but to focus on economics is to miss the point. Behind the large-scale producers of pecorino are one hundred thousand shepherds, many still milking by hand hundreds of sheep a day. Even if they sell the milk, most shepherds retain a profound connection to the cheese and make a few rounds of pecorino for friends and family. And I am sure these lucky recipients do as my father did, proudly presenting their shepherd's pecorino the way Americans might show off a new car.

Such is the importance of pecorino to our people—each smell and taste reflecting a part of the land. Tinkling sheep bells are the island's soundtrack, their music filling every hill and mountainside as they have for centuries. No wonder we literally keep the cheese close to our hearts: like most Sardinian women, my mother always has a piece of pecorino cheese in her apron to stave off hunger or to offer to a child as a snack. It is the soul of our culinary traditions—our meals begin and end with pecorino; our pantries are filled with it any time of year. For more on cheese in Sardinia, see page 84.

Bottarga with celery and tomatoes
Buttariga kin Sellere a Issalata

SERVES 4

My favorite days growing up were when my father and Zio Valerio would take me down to the beach to fish. Orosei is not a port, but our gulf and beaches are spectacular and the waters are popular with some townspeople and fishermen for fishing, especially for catching lobsters and shellfish. We'd get to the beach early, set up a cabana, and build a fire. As we caught, cleaned, and cooked our catch for lunch, my father and my uncle would always welcome a few of the fishermen to our "table" and in return they would offer fish from their catch and slices of what looked like a flat orange salami. This is when, at the age of three, I first tried bottarga di muggine, the Sardinian caviar made from the roe of grey mullet. I think this salad—versions of which can be found all over Sardinia—is perfect for your first bottarga experience. Light, crisp, and easy to prepare, this dish will take you directly to our shores. The traditional recipe calls for both grated and whole bottarga, but whole bottarga can be harder to find outside of Sardinia. Do all you can to find it (and make sure you peel back the outer skin or sac before shaving). If you cannot find whole bottarga, prepare the salad with an extra sprinkling of grated bottarga over the finished salad.

◇　◇　◇

Chop the celery stalks into thin slices on the diagonal. Coarsely chop the tender leaves, discarding any tough or wilted leaves.

In a large bowl, combine celery and tomatoes. Add 2 tablespoons of the olive oil and the grated bottarga. Sprinkle with salt and pepper. Toss well.

Divide among four plates and top with shavings of whole bottarga. Drizzle with the remaining tablespoon of olive oil to finish.

1 celery heart

1 cup teardrop tomatoes (or cherry tomatoes), halved

3 tablespoons fruttato extra virgin olive oil (see page 40)

1½ teaspoons grated bottarga di muggine (see page 30)

Sea salt and freshly ground black pepper

1 ounce whole bottarga di muggine (see page 30), thinly sliced

BOTTARGA: THE SARDINIAN CAVIAR

Buttariga (or *bottarga*—bow-TAR-gah—in Italian) is the salted, pressed, and air-dried fish roe known as the Sardinian caviar; it dates back at least three thousand years to the beginning of civilization on the island (and possibly to prehistoric times). In truth, the curing process that preserves the roe is not purely Sardinian in origin; it could be found in Roman-Jewish kitchens and has an ancient history in Sicily, Turkey, Greece, Egypt, parts of the Arabian empire, and even Japan. But Sardinian fishermen, working hard to preserve the traditional methods and maintain high production values in the face of increased demand, are widely acknowledged as the masters of this art and the keepers of this tradition today.

Sardinian bottarga, which looks like a long, flat orange sausage, is traditionally made from grey mullet and called bottarga di muggine. (Bottarga is also made from tuna, which has a much stronger flavor than mullet and is less popular in Sardinia.) The fish for bottarga are usually caught in September and October. First, the long, fat roe sack is carefully removed whole. Then, it is cured in salt to remove any moisture, pressed gently under weighted boards, and air dried for around a month, during which it is hand-rubbed to eliminate air pockets.

The result is a lusty, salty distillation of the sea that is revered in Sardinia. Served thinly sliced or grated, a small amount provides a world of flavor to intradas, pastas, and more. And it will stay fresh for months when wrapped well. Try a slice of bottarga on its own with a glass of white wine, on a piece of crusty bread with some olive paste and butter, or mix a little grated bottarga with ricotta and spread on a piece of pane carasau.

Fennel and crabmeat salad with bottarga
Cavaru a Issalata kin Inucru e Buttariga

SERVES 4

I love to introduce guests to bottarga with this salad. It also showcases the quality of a good Sardinian extra virgin olive oil, in this case, fruttato olive oil. The fruttato oil and bottarga mix with the crabmeat, oranges, and fennel (which grows wild in the hills of Orosei) to make a salad that has a texture as interesting as its ingredients. It is also a great make-ahead recipe as the flavor is just as good the next day.

Prepare the fennel by cutting it in half lengthwise, removing the core, very thinly slicing the bulb, and finely chopping the fennel fronds. Set the chopped fronds aside.

In a small bowl, mix half of the fruttato olive oil, half of the lemon juice, and freshly ground black pepper to taste. Pour mixture over the sliced fennel, tossing well to evenly coat.

Pick through the crabmeat, checking for pieces of shell. Place crabmeat in a bowl with tomatoes, green onions, chopped fennel fronds, lemon and orange zests, and grated bottarga. Toss well to combine.

Plate sliced fennel on the serving plate and top with the crabmeat mixture and orange sections. Drizzle with the remaining ¼ cup of fruttato olive oil and lemon juice.

1 large head fennel

½ cup fruttato extra virgin olive oil (see page 40)

1 lemon, juice and 1 teaspoon grated zest

Freshly ground black pepper

½ pound lump crab meat

2 Roma tomatoes, seeded, drained, and diced

4 green onions, sliced, white and light green parts only

1 orange, sections and 2 teaspoons grated zest

1 to 2 tablespoons grated bottarga di muggine (see page 30)

SARDINIA AND OLIVE OIL

Olive trees are everywhere on the island and produce some of the finest oils in the world. When I was growing up, most families in Orosei had at least an olive tree or two that they had used for generations to make their own oil. In the fall, we would harvest the olives and bring them to the local *mulino* (or mill) where granite wheels seven feet tall and three feet wide would press the olives flat. They were then stacked on cloth frames and hot water would pour down to separate the oil. The mill would keep a portion of each family's oil as a fee (what we called a "ransom"). Today, the magnificence of the whole process—from the huge granite wheels, to the procession of families coming in with their olives and leaving with these beautiful urns of oil—has been replaced by sterile machines. But olive oil remains essential in Sardinia.

Bottarga and raw artichokes
Buttariga kin Carzoffeddas e Ozu Novu
SERVES 4

My family uses artichokes in almost everything: as a side dish or as an ingredient in pastas, soups, stews, grilled dishes, fish, and roasts. In Sardinia, the best and the biggest artichokes of the season arrive in January and grow in the middle of the stalks. To us, these artichokes mean spring is around the corner. We would head to the flatlands by the Cedrino River to pick them and eat them raw—yes, I said raw—with a little olive oil and salt we would keep in our pockets. (We also peel and eat artichoke stems and I flinch every time I see one thrown away.) I also love raw artichokes in a salad like this one with bottarga, which combines the flavors of land and sea and offers a fresh way of using these traditional ingredients. I use a novello olive oil (the first oil of the season available in late December or January), which gives the salad a bright, earthy but still delicate flavor.

◊ ◊ ◊

Clean and trim artichokes; cut lengthwise into quarters. Remove the choke, leaving the heart and tender bottom leaves. Place the quarters directly into a bowl of cold water with half of the lemon juice to prevent artichokes from turning black.

In a small bowl, combine remaining lemon juice and the novello olive oil.

Drain the quartered artichokes and pat dry; cut into very thin slices. Toss with enough dressing to coat, reserving any leftover dressing. Season with a pinch of sea salt and freshly ground black pepper to taste. Combine well so artichokes are evenly coated.

Gently mix in the bottarga slices. Drizzle with any remaining dressing before serving.

6 medium artichokes
Juice of 1 lemon
½ cup novello extra virgin olive oil (or fruttato extra virgin olive oil, see page 40)
Sea salt and freshly ground black pepper
6 ounces whole bottarga di muggine (see page 30), thinly shaved

ARTICHOKES

Artichokes have been a staple of the Mediterranean diet for centuries, and Italy has long produced the most artichokes in the world. Italian immigrants even cultivated the first American artichokes in California in the nineteenth century. In Italy, Sardinia and Sicily produce the most artichokes, with the Sardinian varieties considered to be among the finest anywhere. Within Sardinia, Orosei and Oristano are the largest producers of artichokes. Both the wild spiny and cultivated globe varieties (we prefer the spiny kind; the mainland prefers the smooth ones) thrive on the flatlands by our rivers alongside asparagus, peas, fava beans, mushrooms, and watermelons. I also grew up alongside those artichokes, and I could not be happier about their worldwide acclaim.

Crab with garlic and pepperoncino
Cavaros a Buddittu

SERVES 4

When I come home to Sardinia, the first trip I make after seeing my parents is to visit our olive trees that overlook the ocean. The smell of the sea alerts me that I am home, and the taste of salt in the air takes me back to moments when I was a boy. Eating clams, mussels, and octopus do this to me, as do the tiny granchi di fiume (a variety of crab), which are found along the rocks in the rivers and sea. We would catch them, boil them in sea water, and dig in. We had to get our hands dirty and work hard to get the meat from the small, crunchy crabs, but it was worth it. This recipe is more complex than boiled crab but remains close to basics. I like the garlicky spicy taste, which enhances the crab flavor and makes great cooking juices for dipping bread. You'll need to substitute blue crabs for the granchi di fiume to get a similar result.

◇　◇　◇

Bring salted water to a boil in a stock pot. Add crabs and boil for 6 to 8 minutes; remove and set aside to cool.

If using blue crabs, when crabs are cool enough to handle, remove top shell and legs and discard. Cut remaining crab bodies in half along the middle.

In a large saucepan, heat olive oil over medium heat. Add garlic and pepperoncino and cook until garlic is softened. Add crab, parsley, and sea salt to taste. Sauté for 5 minutes. Add white wine and simmer for a few minutes for flavors to penetrate.

Serve with a cracking utensil. This dish is excellent served hot or cold.

2 pounds granchi di fiume (or 8 female blue crabs)
½ cup extra virgin olive oil
6 garlic cloves, minced
1 whole fresh pepperoncino, halved (or ½ teaspoon crushed red pepper flakes)
1 bunch flat leaf parsley, finely chopped
Sea salt
¼ cup Vermentino wine (or other dry white wine)

Calamari with fresh artichokes
Calamares e Carzoffeddas

SERVES 4

By the warm days of June, artichokes are so abundant that the smells of them cooking escape from every home, filling the streets of Orosei. Some we preserve in our own oil for winter, especially the carciofini (baby artichokes). Some we eat in salads or plain with just a squeeze of lemon and salt or simmered in white wine. This soup is something different and embodies the Sardinian love of combining two ingredients that are not often thought of together (but that are very easy to find and not too expensive) to create something new. This is essentially the same recipe my mother made when I was growing up.

In a large pot over medium heat, sauté garlic in olive oil until golden brown. Add artichokes and sauté for 5 minutes longer. Add the calamari and let tenderize for a few minutes.

Add the wine and simmer until the alcohol is evaporated. Stir in the tomatoes and chopped parsley until combined. Season with salt and pepper to taste. Add fish stock and bring to a boil. Reduce heat and simmer for 15 minutes.

Divide among four shallow bowls and garnish each with a sprig of parsley.

2 garlic cloves, thinly sliced

2 tablespoons extra virgin olive oil

2 artichoke hearts, cleaned and thinly sliced

1 pound calamari rings

¼ cup Vermentino wine (or other dry white wine)

2 Roma tomatoes, seeded and diced

1 bunch flat leaf parsley, finely chopped, with 4 sprigs reserved for garnish

Sea salt and freshly ground black pepper

5 cups fish stock (see recipe, page 68)

CLEANING ARTICHOKES

Artichokes must be cleaned and trimmed before cooking, but they will turn brown almost as soon as they are cut, so make sure you have a bowl of water with some lemon juice standing by to stop the browning. To clean artichokes down to the bottom or "heart," rotate the artichoke and snap off (or cut with a paring knife) the tough, dark outer leaves until you have reached the light, tender leaves inside. Next, cut off only the end of the stem and peel off its rough fibrous exterior. Now, cut off the top of the artichoke about one third from the top point. Finally, scoop out the inedible inner choke with a pointed spoon and drop the artichoke into the lemon-water bath. You now have a whole artichoke heart ready to use. (Note: Baby artichokes don't have a thorny choke and need only their tops, bottoms, and outer leaves trimmed.)

Calamari stuffed with ricotta and bottarga
Calamare Prenu

SERVES 4

My sister Angela lives in the ancient city of Nuoro, which sits high on a giant ridge west of Monte Ortobene. Often called the heart of inland Sardinian culture, Nuoro lacks the cosmopolitan energy of the ports of Oristano or Olbia and feels more like what it is: a city created by descendents of our finest shepherds. Yet Nuoro is also home to our finest artists, including our best-known poet (Sebastiano Satta) and contemporary writer (Salvatore Satta), and Grazia Deledda, winner of the Nobel Prize for Literature in 1926 (see page 103). Angela's house is in the beautiful old city, where you can actually find pieces of poetry tacked to the exterior walls of buildings. I went to high school in this literary town, and my sister often cooked for me. This dish of hers is like Nuoro itself, a mix of old ingredients and new ideas. It blends the flavors of the land she lives in now with those of the sea she grew up with in Orosei. Salty and briny, creamy and complex, it is a combination that might inspire poetry.

◊ ◊ ◊

Separate the calamari bodies from the tentacles. Rinse the bodies thoroughly under cold running water and set aside. Finely chop tentacles.

In a medium bowl, mix chopped calamari, capers, olives, parsley, pecorino, bread crumbs, and garlic. Stir in 1 tablespoon of olive oil and then the egg. In a small bowl, combine ricotta with 2 tablespoons of grated bottarga.

Gently fold the ricotta mixture into the calamari mixture. Fill the calamari bodies about three-quarters full of the mixture and secure closed with a toothpick.

Preheat oven to 350°F.

Heat 1 tablespoon of olive oil in a medium skillet over medium heat. Add stuffed calamari and brown evenly. Place browned calamari in a baking dish and bake for 15 minutes.

In the same skillet, heat remaining 2 tablespoons olive oil and the anchovies. Stir continuously with a wooden spoon until anchovies dissolve. Add the butter and 2 tablespoons of grated bottarga. Stir often with a wooden spoon to prevent burning.

Serve calamari topped with the sauce and sprinkle with the remaining bottarga.

8 whole calamari

1 tablespoon capers, drained

2 tablespoons finely chopped pitted Kalamata olives

2 tablespoons finely chopped flat leaf parsley

½ cup grated Pecorino Sardo cheese (or other pecorino cheese)

½ cup bread crumbs

2 garlic cloves, finely chopped

4 tablespoons extra virgin olive oil

1 egg

1 cup sheep's milk ricotta cheese (or other creamy ricotta cheese)

½ cup grated bottarga di muggine (see page 30)

2 anchovies

1 tablespoon butter

Salad of arugula, pears, ricotta salata, and walnuts
Issalata Ortobene

SERVES 4

My brother Francesco and I celebrated our parents' "Nozze d'Oro," or golden (50th) anniversary, by re-creating a wedding meal for our entire family in their honor at Su Barchile, my family's inn in Orosei. In preparation for the meal, we combed our father's olive orchards and walked the Cedrino River to pick wild asparagus, dandelions, arugula, and herbs. Then we spotted the pear trees my father kept in his yard and knew we had to make at least one dish with pears in it. My father loves pears, and my brother and I created this salad the day of the party to evoke a taste of the land he had known all his life. The sweet pears, spicy arugula, bitter endive, salty cheese, and crunchy walnuts make an earthy and delicious combination. Serve this salad when the pears come in during fall and winter—a fall/winter counterpart to the spring/summer watermelon salad on page 39.

◇　◇　◇

Core the pears, leaving the skin on. Slice into thin rings. Lay pears on plates.

In a bowl, toss arugula and Belgian endive with ¼ cup olive oil. Mound the mixture on the pears.

Top salad with walnuts and ricotta salata. Season with salt and pepper to taste and drizzle with remaining tablespoon of olive oil.

2 pears

½ pound arugula, cleaned well and coarsely chopped

1 head Belgian endive, thinly sliced

¼ cup plus 1 tablespoon single-orchard extra virgin olive oil (see page 40)

½ cup chopped walnuts

½ cup coarsely grated ricotta salata cheese

Sea salt and freshly ground black pepper

SA ESTA E SAN'ANTONI E S'OCCU

My parents' "Nozze d'Oro," coincided with one of the most sacred festivals in Sardinia: Sa Esta e san'Antoni e s'Occu (the Feast of St. Anthony). Every January 16 at 5:30 p.m., huge bonfires traditionally made of fresh rosemary branches are lit all across the island. According to legend, the abbot St. Anthony, the patron saint of all four-legged creatures, journeyed to Hell, battled the devil, and stole his burning coal, returning to the surface to warm the people and the land. The bonfires lit in his honor symbolize the warming of the earth for seeds and offer hope for a bountiful harvest in the year to come.

In Orosei, the entire town comes together to join in building the fire in the courtyard in front of the tower of St. Anthony. The tower has withstood numerous attacks, including the brutal raids of the Barbareschi pirates, who were driven back by the townspeople in 1806. As plumes of fragrant smoke rise to the skies, the local bishop leads the townspeople in a procession around the edges of the fire, circling three times to be "purified" and begin the New Year cleansed. Atop the branches sits a cross, covered with oranges. The boys from the town (some as young as twelve, who have waited to be old enough for this chance) race to find a safe path among the smoldering branches so that they can pull down the oranges. The town cheers as they throw the fruit to the younger children below. Everyone talks and sings and dances and drinks through the night. Then, of course, we eat.

Watermelon salad with arugula, ricotta salata, and walnuts
Sindria a Issalata
SERVES 4

This salad is a natural combination for me: in Orosei, bitter greens like arugula and dandelion grow alongside watermelons. Every summer, my brothers and I walked to the river to pick watermelons just as my father had taught us, looking for only the ripest fruit with mature (dry) stems. We piled them proudly by the riverbank and waited for my father to come, watching as he inspected and then tapped each one and listened for the hollow echo that meant they were ripe. Pocketknife at the ready, he then cut a triangle about two inches wide, tasted it, and said the words we loved to hear: "This is beautiful." So is this salad. The refreshing, cool sweetness of the watermelon and creamy ricotta salata is balanced by the peppery bitterness of the arugula and the crunch of red onions and walnuts. Today, I like to enhance this salad of my youth with the sweet/tangy flavor of raspberry vinegar.

◇ ◇ ◇

Remove the inside of the watermelon and cut into 1-inch cubes. Combine watermelon, arugula, and red onion in a large bowl. Refrigerate for 1 hour.

In a separate bowl, mix the raspberry vinegar, lime juice, and orange juice. Refrigerate for 1 hour.

Remove from refrigerator and combine watermelon mixture and vinegar mixture. Season with salt and pepper to taste.

Divide among four plates and drizzle with any dressing that remains in the bowl. Top with the walnuts and ricotta. Finish with a drizzling of olive oil.

1 large chunk seedless watermelon (about 1 pound)
1½ cups coarsely chopped arugula
1 small red onion, sliced into thin rings
2 tablespoons raspberry vinegar
Juice of 1 lime
Juice of 1 small orange
Sea salt and freshly ground black pepper
1 cup chopped walnuts
2 ounces coarsely grated ricotta salata
1 to 2 tablespoons extra virgin olive oil

FINISHING OILS

Most Sardinians have at least two oils in their pantries—one for cooking and one for finishing. Finishing oils are generally of a higher quality and contain more subtle flavor notes that would go unnoticed if the oil were cooked into a dish. They are used to impart flavor, not necessarily to add to the unctuousness of a dish. You might think of them in the same way you think of truffle oil or chile oil; the oil is a means of conveying flavor, not a cooking medium. This is why I often will recommend a specific type of oil for use at the end of a recipe, separate from the standard "extra virgin olive oil" used for cooking throughout.

Fruttato is one essential type of finishing oil used in Sardinia. Literally, fruttato means "fruity," and this oil retains a strong taste of the fruit—the olive itself—because the olives for fruttato are picked just as they reach maturity. This oil also has a lower acidity than most. In Sardinia, fruttato oil displays to great effect the nuances that result from the island's rich volcanic soil.

Fruttato and other finishing oils are like wine—they tend to display individual characteristics based on where the olives were grown, how they were grown, and the method of production. If an olive oil is labeled "organic," chances are it is of a higher quality since special care was taken in maintaining the olive trees. If an oil's label indicates it comes from a single orchard, then a high level of quality is generally guaranteed. So, sometimes I will call for a "single-orchard olive oil" in this book. These are instances when fruitiness is not as desirable as a deeper earthier flavor is.

I drizzle almost every dish I eat with a bit of a finishing olive oil. I encourage you to experiment with a couple different types of finishing oils and see which you like best. What is labeled as "extra virgin olive oil" in most supermarkets can be of widely ranging quality. Many oils are blends from many different orchards and even from different countries! Look for "fruttato," "organic," and/or "single orchard" on the label and you're likely to find something worth using as a finishing oil. These oils of course tend to cost more, but you use less of them, and the taste is worth it!

Cold seafood salad
Issalata de Iscolliu

SERVES 4

Shellfish, which lives on or close to the shore, has been a part of Sardinian cuisine for centuries. Clams, mussels, snails, shrimp, lobster, and crab of remarkable variety thrive in our waters. Thus, everyone who lives along the coast of Sardinia has a recipe for seafood salad, and every cook has his or her own personal way of making it. Two sisters growing up in the same town might have different recipes. One might be beholden to her dressing and guided by what was available in the market that day for the seafood. The other one might be adamant that the combination of shellfish be precise or the salad would not be worth making. This is my favorite recipe. I'm like the second sister; I like this precise balance of shellfish–but feel free to follow the first sister's lead and adjust the ingredients based on what is available in your market. This salad makes a perfect summer party dish, especially as it can be made a day ahead and refrigerated. The key is freshness: use only shellfish that is in season and as fresh as possible.

◇　◇　◇

Steam mussels and clams until opened. Remove mussels and clams from shells. Discard shells.

Boil the shrimp and calamari in salted water for 2 minutes. Transfer to a bowl of ice water to cool.

Combine shrimp, calamari, mussels, and clams in a medium bowl. Stir in ¼ cup of olive oil and citrus juices. Cover tightly and refrigerate for at least 1 hour before serving.

Prior to serving, drizzle with fruttato olive oil and add salt and pepper to taste.

1 pound mussels
1 pound clams
½ pound shrimp, peeled and deveined
½ pound calamari rings
¼ cup extra virgin olive oil
Juice of 1 medium lime
Juice of 1 medium lemon
Sea salt and freshly ground black pepper
1 to 2 tablespoons fruttato extra virgin
    olive oil

Shrimp with orange and chicory
Cambaros kin Frutta

SERVES 4

I *always say the simplicity of Sardinian cuisine, both old and new, is deceiving. Take this dish, which combines a few typical Sardinian ingredients to create a modern but quintessentially Sardinian take on shrimp salad. Traditionally, we just throw shrimp on a fire and toss it with olive oil and some citrus. One day, I was looking at the orange trees that fill my parents' yard and the town and flatlands of Orosei, and I thought of adding the actual oranges, not just the juice, to the shrimp. To offset the oranges' sweetness, I added chicory, one of the bitter greens that grow wild all over Sardinia. If you never had chicory—or never knew what to do with it when you did have it—try it in this salad. it has spicy bite but not enough to hide the deeper sweetness.*

◊   ◊   ◊

Boil shrimp in salted water for 2 to 3 minutes. Transfer to a bowl of ice water to cool and stop the cooking process.

Combine shrimp, oranges, and chicory. Add the olive oil and gently toss. Cover and refrigerate at least 1 hour before serving to combine flavors.

Divide shrimp and orange mixture among four plates and drizzle with the remaining juices.

In a small bowl, stir lime juice and mosto d'uva and drizzle on salad before serving.

1½ pounds medium shrimp, peeled and deveined

2 medium oranges, peeled and cut in ½-inch cubes

½ pound chicory, coarsely chopped

½ cup extra virgin olive oil

Juice of 2 limes

1 tablespoon mosto d'uva

MOSTO D'UVA AND SABA

Sardinia shares with the mainland the ancient, meticulous craft of reducing grape must (or unfermented grape juice) in large copper pots into a rich, not-too-sweet liquid called mosto d'uva (in Sardo, *vinu cottu*) or even further (with the addition of sugar and sometimes orange or lemon rinds) into syrup called saba (in Sardo, *sapa*).

Like everything in Sardinia, the making of mosto d'uva is seasonal and must be done before the grapes begin to ferment and winter comes. I prefer varieties using the hearty Carignano grape (grown in the southwest of the island), which, like the more recognized Cannonau, was brought by the Phoenicians. Mosto d'uva is like balsamic vinegar without the acidity. Sardinians use it to add a hint of sweetness to everything from intradas to *durke* (desserts). Saba is more concentrated than mosto d'uva and was originally created for our pastries and other desserts, but we now serve it with meats and in sauces.

Jumbo shrimp and scampi with zucchini
Iscampos e Cambaros
SERVES 4

More delicate and harder to find than lobster, scampi is a real treat in Sardinia. It is found in the cold waters near ports like Arbatax. That's where Zia Maria first discovered scampi roasted over a fire with some salt and citrus. She never forgot it and has served it as a summertime special in her restaurant for thirty years. So for my parents' golden wedding anniversary, my brother Francesco and I knew we had to drive to Arbatax to find a fisherman with scampi and shrimp to create a special dish. Usually scampi heads and claws are left on during cooking, but in preparing this dish, my brother and I removed the heads, lightly floured and fried them, and then used them as garnish. But with or without the heads, this dish makes a wonderful hors d'oeuvre for entertaining. If you cannot find scampi or langoustine, you can use all jumbo shrimp.

◇　◇　◇

In a small bowl, whisk together ½ cup of olive oil, lemon juice, vinegar, dill, and parsley. Season to taste with salt and pepper.

Slice the zucchini and squash lengthwise into long strips about ⅛ inch thick.

Preheat oven to 350°F. Peel and devein shrimp and scampi, leaving tails on. Place in a large bowl and toss with marinade until coated evenly. Set aside for 5 minutes.

Starting from the tail, wrap a vegetable strip around one shrimp, spiraling toward the head end. Continue wrapping until entire shrimp is covered. Use about 4 strips for each shrimp or scampi. Alternate vegetables as you like. Continue with the remaining shrimp and scampi until all are fully wrapped.

Brush the bottom of a baking dish with the 2 remaining tablespoons of olive oil. Place the shrimp and scampi into the baking dish. Drizzle with any remaining marinade. Cook in the preheated oven for 10 minutes, until the shrimp and scampi are pink and firm to the touch.

Arrange the shrimp and scampi on a serving dish and drizzle with remaining cooking liquids.

½ cup plus 2 tablespoons extra virgin olive oil
¼ cup lemon juice
2 teaspoons balsamic vinegar
2 tablespoons finely chopped dill
2 tablespoons finely chopped flat leaf parsley
Sea salt and freshly ground black pepper
1 medium zucchini
1 medium yellow squash
8 jumbo shrimp, heads removed
8 scampi (or baby langoustine), heads removed

SHRIMP AND SCAMPI

Shrimp are shrimp, that's easy. Prawns are shrimp, too, with larger shrimp often called prawns to distinguish them from the "shrimps." Just what are scampi? In North America, scampi is usually a dish in an Italian restaurant featuring shrimp cooked with garlic and butter, but scampi in Sardinia is an actual crustacean—a relative of the shrimp known commonly as the "Dublin Bay prawn." Scampi look like shrimp but with pincer claws similar to a lobster or French langoustine.

Cuttlefish and peas
Seppia kin Pisellu
SERVES 4

In Orosei and all over Sardinia, cuttlefish is readily available and not too expensive. It turns up in dozens of traditional Sardinian recipes on its own or cut up in a seafood salad. This springtime recipe is based on my mother's, who learned from her mother that cuttlefish and peas are a natural combination. "Abbaita sa terra e su mare," she would tell me. ("Look to the land and look to the sea.") "Ask what two flavors go together." In this case, both main ingredients have a delicate, sweet taste that make this dish say "Spring."

◇   ◇   ◇

If using whole, fresh cuttlefish, clean thoroughly. Remove bone, eyes, and beak. If necessary, remove outer skin. Rinse tentacles especially well to remove sand and other impurities. Cut cuttlefish into 1-inch (bite-size) pieces.

In a large pot over medium heat, bring stock to a rolling boil.

Heat olive oil in a saucepan over medium heat. Add garlic and onion and sauté for 2 to 3 minutes. Add cuttlefish, raise heat to high, and sauté for 3 to 5 minutes. Add wine and let simmer for 2 minutes, until most of the liquid is absorbed. Reduce heat to medium

1 pound cuttlefish
2 to 3 cups vegetable stock
3 tablespoons extra virgin olive oil
2 garlic cloves, chopped
1 extra large green onion, coarsely chopped
¼ cup Vermentino wine (or other dry white wine)
1 bunch flat leaf parsley, coarsely chopped
Sea salt
1 pound fresh peas, shelled (or frozen)

low and add parsley, a pinch of salt, and hot vegetable stock to cover mixture. Cover and simmer for 5 minutes. Add the peas and cook for 10 minutes longer, stirring occasionally.

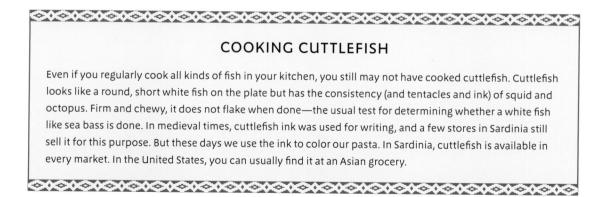

COOKING CUTTLEFISH

Even if you regularly cook all kinds of fish in your kitchen, you still may not have cooked cuttlefish. Cuttlefish looks like a round, short white fish on the plate but has the consistency (and tentacles and ink) of squid and octopus. Firm and chewy, it does not flake when done—the usual test for determining whether a white fish like sea bass is done. In medieval times, cuttlefish ink was used for writing, and a few stores in Sardinia still sell it for this purpose. But these days we use the ink to color our pasta. In Sardinia, cuttlefish is available in every market. In the United States, you can usually find it at an Asian grocery.

Roasted sardines
Sardinas kin Azu

SERVES 4

Yes, *all jokes aside, you can get sardines in Sardinia. They are so abundant they may have been named after the island (not the other way around). Delicious and inexpensive, they also cook quickly and easily: my mother would cook literally a hundred or more at once—enough for everyone at the table to have at least twenty. (Their high oil content means any leftover sardines can be reheated without drying out.) We'd have them for lunch or dinner with some soup or cheese. And since they were small and require a little work to eat, they also kept the children busy at the table. If you have never prepared fresh sardines before, this is the recipe to start. It makes a great appetizer or even a light meal.*

⬦　⬦　⬦

Clean sardines thoroughly, making sure to remove gills and insides. (Or, you can ask your fishmonger to do this.) Rinse under running water to wash off scales or remaining blood.

Preheat oven to 350°F. Coat the bottom of a sheet pan with half of the extra virgin olive oil. Place sardines parallel to one another on the sheet pan, close but not touching one another. Evenly sprinkle garlic and parsley over the sardines.

In a small bowl, combine remaining extra virgin olive oil and lemon juice. Drizzle evenly over the sardines. Sprinkle with the sea salt.

Place in oven and cook for 5 minutes. Pour white wine over sardines and finish cooking in the oven for 5 minutes longer.

2 pounds fresh sardines, with scales rubbed off
1 cup extra virgin olive oil
8 garlic cloves, thinly sliced
1 bunch flat leaf parsley, coarsely chopped
Juice of 1 lemon
1 teaspoon coarse sea salt
¼ cup Vernaccia wine (or other dry white wine)

Octopus salad for the Festival of Saint Maria of the Sea
Purpu de Santa Maria

SERVES 4

This is an octopus salad for Orosei's Festa di Santa Maria del Mare, or the Festival of Saint Maria of the Sea, which happens every year on the last Sunday in May. Some Sardinian festivals (such as those honoring Saint Anthony or my namesake, Saint Efisio, the patron saint of Sardinia) are celebrated all over the island. But many festivals happen in only a few towns. La Festa di Santa Maria del Mare is one such festival. (Besides the one in Orosei, I know of only one other, in Bosa, near Oristano.) Our festival dates to the Middle Ages. It starts in the early morning when everyone gathers in the center of town, where boats have been decorated from bow to stern with flowers. We then walk them to the Cedrino River to start an elaborate procession on the river where people line the shore and cheer. As you might expect, the festival is incomplete without a meal. We finish with a lunch of sandwiches and fish dishes like this garlicky octopus salad.

◈　◈　◈

If using whole, fresh octopus, clean thoroughly. Remove eyes and beak; turn inside out and discard viscera. Rinse under cold running water, checking tentacles especially well for sand and other impurities.

In a stock pot, bring 6 to 8 cups of water and the vinegar to a boil. Add octopus and boil for 30 minutes. Turn off heat and let it sit for 15 minutes for octopus to continue to absorb flavors. Remove and immediately immerse octopus in a bowl filled with ice water to stop cooking. Pat octopus dry and cut into ¾-inch pieces. Refrigerate for at least 1 hour.

In a small bowl, mix lemon juice with the parsley and garlic. Refrigerate until ready to use.

Prior to serving, add lemon juice mixture to octopus and toss to combine. Add olive oil and salt and pepper to taste. Toss well and serve.

> 1 pound octopus
> 1 tablespoon red wine vinegar
> Juice of 1 lemon
> ¼ cup finely chopped flat leaf parsley
> 4 garlic cloves, minced
> ¼ cup extra virgin olive oil
> Sea salt and freshly ground black pepper

Octopus with new potatoes and red onion
Purpu Acru-Durke
SERVES 4

When I was twelve years old, I went with Zio Pietro to the rocky coast north of town to hunt for shellfish. First, I helped my uncle build a fire. Then, we combed the rocks, prying snails, limpids, and abalone from them with our pocketknives. Next, we attached a white rag to the end of a stick to catch octopus. Drawn to the irresistible white in the water, the octopus would grab onto the rag and we lifted it into our buckets. Then, we would return to the fire and cook all of it, enjoying a seaside meal. Nowadays octopus is harder to find. They are scared away from the shore by the boats (the price we pay for being "discovered"), but we still eat a lot of them. This dish is one of those land-sea combinations I adore. The potatoes and octopus come together to create a flavorsome and substantial appetizer—a cold-weather dish that is simple enough to make at home, but complex enough for Zia Maria to serve at her restaurant at my family's inn, Su Barchile.

◇ ◇ ◇

If using whole, fresh octopus, clean thoroughly. Remove eyes and beak; turn inside out and discard viscera. Rinse under cold running water, checking tentacles especially well for sand and other impurities.

Put garlic cloves, celery, carrot, onion, bay leaf, sea salt, and peppercorns in a large stock pot. Cover with water. Bring to a boil, then add octopus. Cook for 20 minutes. Turn off heat and let sit for 30 minutes to continue to absorb flavors and cool. Remove octopus from pot and chop into ¼-inch diagonal slices. Refrigerate for at least 1 hour.

Boil the new potatoes, then peel. Set one potato aside and quarter the remaining potatoes. Put quartered potatoes and red onion in a bowl; cover and refrigerate until ready to use.

Add reserved potato, mosto d'uva, olive oil, and balsamic vinegar to a blender. Blend on high to emulsify. Add the emulsion to the octopus and toss well. Let octopus sit for at least 15 minutes before serving. Place the potato and onion mixture on the plate and top with the octopus. Sprinkle with the green onions.

1 pound octopus
4 garlic cloves, whole
1 stalk celery, halved
1 carrot, cut into 2 to 3 large pieces
1 medium white onion, halved
1 bay leaf
1 tablespoon sea salt
1 teaspoon black peppercorns
1 pound new potatoes
½ red onion, thinly sliced
¼ cup mosto d'uva (see page 42)
¼ cup extra virgin olive oil
1 tablespoon balsamic vinegar
2 green onions, green part only, thinly sliced

Eel with fregula and herbs
Ambidda de Riu kin Fregula
SERVES 4

This is my great grandmother's recipe, and I remember watching my grandmother, Mannai Vardeu, preparing it. Just watching–Mannai Vardeu rarely let me help, not even to open a drawer. Instead, I stood back and stared at her strong hands as she chopped the heads off the eels my grandfather had brought from the river. Her version of this soup is what we call su ministru or soup served with small pasta such as fregula. It comes alive with chicken broth, something we did not always have in our home, but Mannai Vardeu kept chickens in her courtyard and always seemed to have a pot of broth nearby.

◇ ◇ ◇

Scrub eel with sea salt to clean, then rinse well under running water. Pat dry and cut into 2- to 3-inch pieces.

Heat 2 tablespoons of the olive oil in a medium saucepan over medium heat. Stir in eel and add salt to taste; cook for 2 minutes. Add garlic and cook until softened. Add tomatoes, parsley, bay leaves, and 1 cup of the chicken stock. Reduce heat to low and let cook for 15 minutes.

Bring remaining 3 cups of chicken stock to a boil in a stock pot, add fregula and bring back to a boil. Reduce heat to medium low and cook for 7 minutes, stirring frequently to prevent sticking.

Gently stir in eel mixture and oregano; let simmer for 5 minutes for flavors to combine.

Remove from heat, then stir in remaining olive oil. Let sit for 5 minutes before serving.

1 pound eels (about ½ inch in diameter), cleaned with heads removed

Sea salt (preferably medium grain)

4 tablespoons extra virgin olive oil

3 garlic cloves, thinly sliced

2 Roma tomatoes, seeded and diced

1 bunch flat leaf parsley, chopped

2 bay leaves

4 cups chicken stock

1½ cups fregula (see page 119)

2 sprigs oregano

COOKING EEL

As in the eel recipes in this book, eel in Sardinia is cooked with the backbone in so that the oil and enzymes in the bones can flavor the dish. When cooked, the meat of the eel flakes right off, leaving the bones intact. We also always cook eel with the skin on; it has an amazing flavor.

Eel in tomato sauce
Ambidda a Cassola

SERVES 4

This recipe reminds me of the time when a rain big enough to flood the Cedrino River kept my father home from his job cutting stone. We were spending the day together as a family when all of a sudden my father stood up and disappeared outside. He came back an hour later with a bag of the freshwater eels that thrive in the rivers of Orosei and all over Sardinia. He handed the bag of live eels proudly to my mother and said, "Here. How about dinner?" We spent the rest of the afternoon cleaning and cooking the eels for dinner. When I was older, my father taught me how to catch eels using worms to bait them just like a fish. The tangy vinegar flavor of this dish is very different from what you may be used to with eel. It cuts the eel's fatty fishy flavor and turns it into a real delicacy.

◇　　◇　　◇

Scrub eel with sea salt to clean, then rinse well under running water. Pat dry and cut into 3- to 4-inch pieces.

Heat the olive oil in a large saucepan over medium heat. Add eel, cooking until evenly browned, turning gently. Season eel with a dash of sea salt and pour in the white wine vinegar, stirring gently and cooking for about 5 minutes. Remove eel and set aside.

Add the onion and garlic to saucepan and cook until softened. Add tomatoes and bay leaves and ½ cup water; simmer over low heat for 15 minutes.

Season the tomato sauce with salt and pepper to taste. Add eel and basil; cover and simmer for 15 minutes longer, stirring occasionally to prevent sticking. Remove from heat and let sit covered for 15 to 20 minutes before serving.

Serve on top of pane carasau pieces.

2 pounds eels (about 1 inch in diameter), cleaned with heads removed

Sea salt (preferably medium grain)

4 tablespoons extra virgin olive oil

½ cup white wine vinegar

½ medium onion, julienned

3 garlic cloves, thinly sliced

8 Roma tomatoes, peeled, seeded, and julienned

3 bay leaves

Freshly ground black pepper

1 sprig basil

4 sheets pane carasau (see page 22), each broken into 4 large pieces

ROASTED EELS

We eat eel everywhere in Sardinia—in a spicy sauce with trout in Oristano, with pecorino in Calgiari—but nowhere quite like in Sedilo. In July, fifty thousand people pack the tiny village for L'Ardia di San Costantino, a festival commemorating Constantine's victory over Maxentious. The main attraction is a fast and dangerous horse race that finishes with a high-speed gallop through a narrow arch. You might be willing to try that before trying this staple of the festival meal: eels from Lago Modeo (a lake near Sedilo), skewered and roasted alive on a spit, their heads thrashing to avoid the hot coals.

Vegetable soup with fresh ricotta
Minestrone kin Recottu

SERVES 4

My mother and sisters can make this refreshing summer minestrone from memory. I need a little help remembering. But we all learned it from watching Mannai Carta create it in her kitchen. I lived most of my childhood in my grandmother's home, and I remember always having a lot of fun helping her cook and hearing my grandfather's stories. When we made this soup, my job was shelling the beans my grandfather brought in fresh from the fields. In fact, all the ingredients in this family-style soup are fresh; it features staples of Sardinian summer produce as well as fresh, creamy ricotta. I sometimes prefer to eat this soup warm with the cold ricotta; the contrast of temperatures gives the flavors extra brightness.

◊   ◊   ◊

Place 6 cups of water in a large stock pot. Add potatoes, zucchini, carrots, celery, cabbage, beans, and sea salt and bring to a rolling boil over medium heat. Once mixture begins to boil, reduce heat to low and simmer for 10 to 15 minutes or until vegetables are easily pierced with a fork.

In a saucepan, heat olive oil over medium heat. Add onion and garlic and cook until softened. Add tomatoes, tomato paste, parsley, and a pinch of salt. When mixture begins to bubble, reduce heat to low and let simmer for 10 to 15 minutes, stirring often to prevent sticking.

Add tomato mixture to stock pot and stir to combine. Divide among serving bowls and top each with a spoonful of fresh ricotta.

4 new potatoes, cubed
1 medium zucchini, cubed
2 medium carrots, cubed
1 stalk celery, sliced
½ head green cabbage, cut into 1-inch ribbons
1 cup shelled fresh cranberry beans
1 teaspoon sea salt
2 to 3 tablespoons extra virgin olive oil
1 white onion, diced
3 garlic cloves, minced
½ pound Roma tomatoes, peeled, seeded, drained, and chopped
2 tablespoons tomato paste
1 bunch parsley, finely chopped
1 cup sheep's milk ricotta cheese (or other creamy ricotta cheese)

Cheese curd with tomatoes and basil
Frue kin Tamates

SERVES 4

W*hen I visit my parents in the summertime, my mother always has this dish ready. She knows that no matter how many courses we eat and no matter the time of day, if the frue comes out I will stay at the table. I will even eat this dish for breakfast—the salty, sweet, and chunky cheese is so incredibly good. I think it kept my wife, Lori, in Sardinia when she first visited. Now she eats it every day during our summer vacation. This recipe is the customary way to serve fresh frue, which has a pleasantly sour taste and a texture somewhere between feta cheese and yogurt.*

In a large bowl, toss tomato wedges and basil with olive oil, a pinch of sea salt, and freshly ground black pepper to taste.

Arrange tomatoes on a plate and top with a large slice of the cheese curd.

3 medium ripe beefsteak tomatoes, cored and cut into wedges

2 sprigs basil, coarsely chopped

4 tablespoons extra virgin olive oil (preferably fruttato, see page 40)

Sea salt and freshly ground black pepper

½ pound frue cheese (or imported, quality feta cheese)

FRUE

Frue is Sardinian cheese curd made from sheep's and goat's milk. It is eaten fresh in a simple tomato salad or in a more solid, saltier, aged form that can transform even the simplest vegetable soup. It dates back to the earliest Sardinian civilizations, and there is even some evidence that it was made in our ancient Nuragic villages (see page 149). Until recently, frue was a summertime treat in Sardinia. The shepherds made it when most of their sheep were pregnant and producing less milk. (Besides, summer is too hot to make pecorino, even if the sheep were accommodating.) Today, thanks to refrigeration, frue is available any time of year, but it is still best in the summer, when most of it is produced.

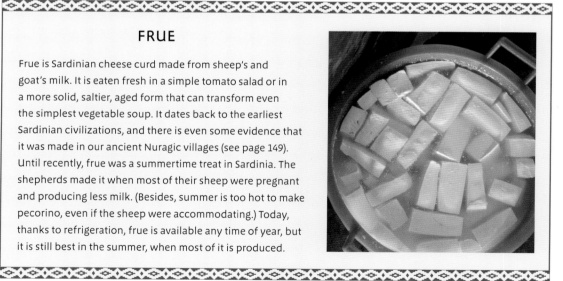

Fregula soup with cheese curd
Minestra e Merca
SERVES 4

My sister Angela made me this soup when I lived with her in Nuoro. She learned the recipe from her husband, Giulio, who is from Nuoro, where frue has been made for more than a thousand years. No wonder this dish is a staple of most local home cooks. Effortless and tasty, the soup uses a frue that has been cured in brine, giving it richness and appealing saltiness. The soup is traditionally made with small short tubular pasta, but I have switched to fregula because it allows more room for the frue, has a fresher taste, and absorbs some of the broth. Enjoy as an intrada or when you need a filling but not heavy meal.

◊　◊　◊

Place potatoes and 5 cups of water in a large stock pot over medium heat and bring to a boil. When the water begins to boil, add fregula and the sea salt. Cook for 8 to 10 minutes, until tender but not mushy.

Remove from heat, stir in olive oil and the frue cheese. Let rest for a few minutes before serving.

¾ pound new potatoes, peeled and cut into ¾- to 1-inch pieces
1 cup fregula (see page 119)
½ teaspoon sea salt
4 tablespoons extra virgin olive oil (preferably one with a spicy flavor)
½ pound aged frue cheese (see page 55) (or a salty feta from brine), cut into ¾-inch cubes

Mixed field greens with figs and goat cheese
Crapinu kin Icu e Issalata Virde

SERVES 4

Figs are everywhere in Sardinia. Buy them in an upscale outdoor market in Porto Cervo or from a cart in Chia—they all will be very good. But my father's figs are magical. Never a farmer by trade, he was given a piece of property with fig trees that had seen better days. Caring for and nurturing them over the course of many years, he became the biggest and best producer of figs in Orosei. He cared so much about the fruit, it would break his heart when he saw visitors peeling the figs before eating them. No matter what we were doing, if he spotted this "atrocity," we would stop so he could demonstrate how to eat a fig properly, biting into it like an apple. I have memories of his trees producing fruit bigger than my hand, some of the figs weighing nearly half a pound. My favorite way to eat figs is straight from the tree. I'll also snack on them with pane carasau and pecorino or with prosciutto and abbamele (see the following recipe, page 58). I also love this salad with its touch of saba but please, for my father's sake, do not peel the figs!

◈　◈　◈

In a large bowl, toss the field greens with the olive oil. Evenly divide among four serving plates.

Arrange figs and goat cheese on top of the greens. Drizzle evenly with the saba. Top with almonds and pepper.

1 pound mixed field greens
¼ cup extra virgin olive oil
8 figs, top and bottom trimmed and cut into wedges
4 ounces goat cheese
4 tablespoons saba (see page 42)
½ cup sliced almonds, toasted
Freshly ground black pepper

Lamb prosciutto with dandelion, figs, and pecorino
Pressuttu de Verveke kin Icu
SERVES 4

I *love the way the figs, dandelion, abbamele, and lamb prosciutto combine with the pecorino in this salad. Wait, did I say lamb prosciutto? Absolutely. Sardinian prosciutto is historically made from the leg of a pig or wild boar. Until recently, to make prosciutto out of anything else would draw incredulous stares from older Sardinians. Why go through all that work curing such a small leg? The next generation has mastered the traditional methods and understands that the same flavors of our land that make our prosciutto taste so good can be applied to different meats to create new Sardinian delicacies. Now the bad news: it is illegal to bring this and most prosciutto into the United States. The good news is many companies and farm stands in America now sell prosciutto made from duck and other game. Feel free to substitute one of these in the recipe.*

◇　◇　◇

Lay shaved prosciutto on platter.

In a small bowl, toss dandelions and figs with ½ cup of olive oil. Mound on top of the prosciutto.

Top with pecorino shavings. Drizzle with remaining olive oil and abbamele.

1 pound lamb prosciutto (or duck magre prosciutto or other wild game prosciutto), thinly shaved

½ pound red dandelion leaves (or chicory), coarsely chopped

4 figs, quartered

1 cup extra virgin olive oil

1 ounce Pecorino Sardo cheese (or other pecorino cheese), thinly shaved

2 tablespoons abbamele

ABBAMELE:
HONEY AND POLLEN REDUCTION

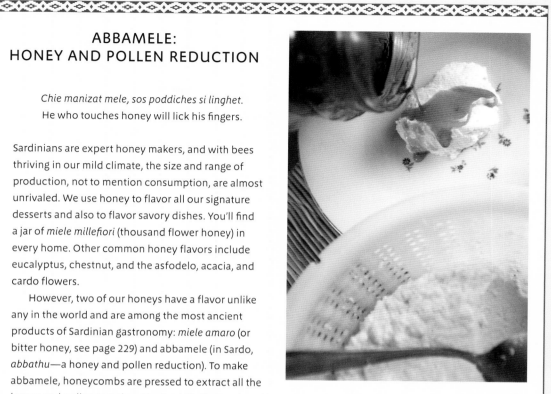

Chie manizat mele, sos poddiches si linghet.
He who touches honey will lick his fingers.

Sardinians are expert honey makers, and with bees thriving in our mild climate, the size and range of production, not to mention consumption, are almost unrivaled. We use honey to flavor all our signature desserts and also to flavor savory dishes. You'll find a jar of *miele millefiori* (thousand flower honey) in every home. Other common honey flavors include eucalyptus, chestnut, and the asfodelo, acacia, and cardo flowers.

However, two of our honeys have a flavor unlike any in the world and are among the most ancient products of Sardinian gastronomy: *miele amaro* (or bitter honey, see page 229) and abbamele (in Sardo, *abbathu*—a honey and pollen reduction). To make abbamele, honeycombs are pressed to extract all the honey and pollen together. The liquid is then reduced in copper pots until a thick, tawny semi-sweet honey is produced. The result is perfect on salads, ice cream, cheese, or fresh fruit.

Breaded mussels on the half shell
Cozzas Arraganatas
SERVES 4

Olbia's fishermen are exceptional. Deep-sea fish such as tuna are a specialty here, whereas the few fishermen among Orosei's shepherds and farmers stuck mostly to freshwater fish and would travel only short distances in the ocean. However, the seafood for which Olbia is renowned are the mussels that come from its gulf's ancient fish farms. The people of Olbia eat these mussels raw or use them in soups, salads, pastas, and more, and you can sample many of these local dishes in May during the city's Festa Manna, or Mussels Fair. One of them will certainly be cozzas arraganatas: mussels shucked fresh and then baked with pecorino-flavored bread crumbs—yes, cheese and fish, one of the few preparations in which you will see the two together. It may be a fisherman's delicacy, but my land-locked children love them.

◈　　◈　　◈

Rinse all mussels thoroughly to remove impurities. Divide mussels, selecting 32 of the largest and reserving the remainder. Use a curved knife to shuck the 32 mussels (similar to shucking an oyster). Place the mussels in the half shell on a baking sheet. Discard empty shells.

Steam the remaining mussels until they open. Discard shells and juices. Chop remaining mussels.

Preheat oven to 350°F.

Mix batter of chopped mussels, parsley, bread crumbs, and half of the pecorino. Season with salt and pepper to taste. In a small bowl, whisk together the mosto d'uva and lemon juice. Add to mussel mixture. Stir in olive oil.

Top raw mussels with the batter mixture. Bake in preheated oven for 10 minutes. Sprinkle with the remaining pecorino and place under the broiler for 1 minute or until golden.

4 pounds mussels
1 bunch flat leaf parsley, finely chopped
1 cup bread crumbs
1 cup finely grated Pecorino Sardo cheese (or other pecorino cheese)
Sea salt and freshly ground black pepper
1 tablespoon mosto d'uva (see page 42)
Juice of 2 lemons
¼ cup extra virgin olive oil

SHUCKING RAW MUSSELS

Using a kitchen towel or glove, hold the mussel tightly with the mouth towards you. Be careful not to squeeze too hard because the shell is very fragile. With your thumb, gently push the upper shell slightly over the bottom shell and insert the tip of a small knife between them. Carefully run the knife around the upper shell, detaching the membrane from the shell and open. Once open, gently loosen the flesh from the top and bottom shell and serve raw with a squeeze of lemon or use to prepare cozzas arraganatas.

RAW SEA URCHIN

In the fall, fisherman in Olbia will surely be seen enjoying another delicacy: sea urchins, shucked fresh, hit with a squeeze of lemon juice, and eaten whole as they squirm from the reaction to the juice. As a teenager, I used to go with friends and gather them from Orosei's rocky coastline. Today, if I am there in season and the moon is full (the full moon is the time to find the fullest sea urchin), I will join friends and local fishermen on the small islands close to Oristano to feast on sea urchins. For those of you not tempted to try them raw, you can try spaghetti with sea urchin (see recipe, page 128).

My father's mussels
Cozzas a sa Moda de Babbu

SERVES 4

My father (pictured below) rarely takes charge in the kitchen or goes to the market. Of course, like any good Sardinian he'll tell you how to grow, pick, hunt or shop for, cook, and eat something, but he leaves the cooking to my mother and grandmothers. Except for this one recipe. Mussels in white wine and garlic are my father's specialty. Whether someone had come back with a few bags of mussels from Olbia or we had just gathered them from the rocks of Orosei, he would get so excited we all just stayed out of his way. First, my father cleaned the mussels in a bucket, spinning them in the water with his hands. I remember this being one of the loudest cooking sounds I have ever heard. My father then picked garlic and parsley and pepperoncino from his garden and headed to the kitchen, where he chopped them roughly and threw them liberally in the pot with some of his own olive oil and Vermentino. Finally, before we ate, he checked each mussel to make sure it had opened.

◈　◈　◈

Rinse mussels thoroughly to remove impurities.

In a stock pot over medium heat, combine olive oil, garlic, and pepperoncino and cook for 2 to 3 minutes. Cut the lemon in half and squeeze each half over the mussels before adding the lemon halves to the pot. Add mussels and parsley.

Stir frequently until mussels start to open. Add wine and keep stirring until all mussels are completely open.

Serve in a ceramic bowl with the pane carasau pieces alongside for dipping into the juices.

3 pounds mussels
½ cup extra virgin olive oil
8 garlic cloves, coarsely chopped
1 fresh pepperoncino, halved (or ½ to 1 teaspoon crushed red pepper)
1 lemon
1 bunch flat leaf parsley, roughly chopped
1 cup Vermentino wine (or other dry white wine)
2 to 3 sheets pane carasau (see page 22), broken into large pieces

Mussels with mirto
Cozzas kin Mirtino

I ate this recipe once at a feast in the countryside of Orosei, and I remember thinking "Why have I not had this before?" As with the songs of the Sardinian countryside, which are often sung unaccompanied by instruments, these ingredients are like voices coming together in beauty. For me, this was an exciting new combination of two classic Sardinian ingredients, mussels and mirto (Sardinian liqueur made from myrtle berries, see page 231). The sweet, nutty flavor of the mirto and a hint of orange really complement the mussels, while the olive oil brings everything together. It tastes like music on a plate.

◇   ◇   ◇

3 pounds mussels
1 orange
¼ cup extra virgin olive oil
6 garlic cloves, cracked
½ cup mirto liqueur (see page 231)

Rinse mussels thoroughly to remove impurities. With a paring knife, cut off the orange zest (the colored part of the peel) in long strips, being careful not to get the bitter white part.

Heat olive oil and garlic in a large skillet over medium-high heat until garlic is softened. Add mussels and sauté for 1 minute. Add 1 cup of warm water and the orange zest. Cover and steam until mussels begin to open, stirring occasionally.

Add mirto liqueur when almost all of the mussels are open. Lower heat and let simmer until sauce becomes syrupy.

Serve mussels in the shell, drizzled with the cooking liquids.

Mussels on the half shell with a spicy tomato relish
Cozzas Piccantes

SERVES 4

When I moved to Texas, I realized with delight that the people on its Gulf Coast share my passion for mussels. It turns out Texans and Sardinians also share a love for all things spicy. This is the Sardinian dish for the Texan in you. The fresh, spicy relish is similar to pico de gallo (and the addition of cilantro a nod to my Texas friends). But the heart is all Sardinian: the olive oil and the sweet-sour flavor of the lime–mosto d'uva mixture combine with the pungent onions, mild mussels, and spicy peppers to make for a unique and delicious cold intrada.

◇ ◇ ◇

Rinse mussels thoroughly to remove impurities.

Steam mussels until open; remove and discard the top shell. Place mussels in the half shell on baking sheets with ½-inch sides.

In a large bowl, combine tomatoes, green onions, Serrano peppers, cilantro, and parsley. In a separate bowl, stir mosto d'uva and lime juice together and pour over the tomato mixture. Toss well to combine and divide evenly over the mussels. Cover with plastic wrap and refrigerate for at least 1 hour.

Drizzle mussels with olive oil before serving. Season with salt to taste.

3 pounds mussels

4 Roma tomatoes, seeded and diced

2 bunches green onions, white and light green parts only, finely chopped

3 green Serrano peppers, seeded and finely chopped

½ bunch cilantro, finely chopped

½ bunch flat leaf parsley, finely chopped

1 teaspoon mosto d'uva (see page 42)

Juice of 3 limes

3 tablespoons extra virgin olive oil

Sea salt

Soup of fregula with baby clams
Fregula kin Arsellas

SERVES 4

This soup is a Sardinian classic. Everywhere on the island, the small hard-shell clams (arselle) thrive in the sand near the water's edge and always have. When I was young, I loved to dig for them at the beach, purging them in a bucket of salt water and taking them home for my mother to make this clam soup. Today, any Sardinian restaurant has this soup on the menu because all Sardinians know it and anyone can make it—and should. It is a great representative of our cuisine and showcases the versatility of one of our signature pastas, fregula. It is also easy to make once you prep the ingredients. Be sure to buy fresh clams that are already purged of sand and impurities. The soup is best presented in a low, wide soup bowl so the clams can be laid around the edges of the dish.

◈   ◈   ◈

Wash clams thoroughly with fresh water. Place clams in a large pot with 1 cup of the stock. Heat until clams open. Remove the clams with a slotted spoon and set aside, keeping warm. Pass cooking liquids through a sieve lined with cheesecloth to remove any sediment and impurities and reserve.

Bring remaining stock to a boil in a saucepan.

Heat ¼ cup of olive oil over medium heat in a large pot (terra-cotta if possible). Add sliced garlic, parsley, and crushed red pepper and sauté until garlic is tender, about 1 minute.

Add the reserved clam juice mixture and boiling stock. Add salt to taste (carefully, since the natural clam juice is already salty). Bring to a boil, add fregula, saffron, and tomatoes and cook 10 minutes on medium heat. Stir frequently to prevent sticking. (Add more stock if broth seems dry.)

Remove pot from heat and stir in lemon zest. Divide clams among bowls, placing clams around rim. Fill with the soup. Drizzle with remaining olive oil.

24 littleneck clams or cockles

5 cups fish stock (see page 68) (or vegetable stock)

¼ cup plus 2 tablespoons extra virgin olive oil

2 garlic cloves, thinly sliced

1 small bunch flat leaf parsley, finely chopped

1 pinch crushed red pepper

Sea salt

1½ cups fregula (see page 119)

1 pinch saffron

3 medium Roma tomatoes, seeded and diced

Grated zest of 1 lemon

Fish stock
Brou de Piske

MAKES ABOUT 6 CUPS

No Sardinian throws away his fish bones; he makes a rich stock first. Ask your fishmonger for these bones and before making the stock, soak them in water and rinse well to remove any blood or impurities (and remove eyes from the heads).

◈　◈　◈

In a large stock pot, heat extra virgin olive oil over medium heat. Add the fish bones, heads, and trimmings and cook for 5 minutes, turning at least once. Add white wine and let liquids evaporate. Add all vegetables and herbs, peppercorns, and salt and pour in water to cover (about 8 cups).

Raise heat to medium-high and bring to a boil. Reduce heat to medium to medium-low and simmer for 30 minutes with lid slightly askew. Remove from heat and let rest for 15 minutes. Filter by passing through a sieve lined with cheesecloth.

4 tablespoons extra virgin olive oil

2 pounds fish bones, heads, and trimmings (preferably from a non-fatty white fish such as red snapper)

½ cup dry white wine

1 stalk celery, cut into 2- to 3-inch pieces

1 leek, white part only, cut into 2- to 3-inch pieces

1 white onion, quartered

Half of 1 fennel bulb

1 Roma tomato, seeded and quartered

3 sprigs thyme

1 bay leaf

1 tablespoon whole white peppercorns

1 teaspoon sea salt

SARDO

You will find this soup of fregula with clams (page 67) everywhere in Sardinia, but like so many quintessential Sardinian dishes, you will find different ingredients or preparations from home to home, town to town. Personally, I like to add a little lemon zest at the end to enhance the flavor of the clams in the broth, but you will not find lemons in other versions.

In this way, our food embodies the same spirit as Sardo, the first language of Sardinia. The official language of the island is Italian, but Sardo with its old Latin, Phoenician, Etruscan, and Catalan roots is our national language. Owing to its long oral history, Sardo was not recorded in its own dictionary until the 21st century, but you'll hear most islanders speak it and you'll find it in our songs, signs, and official documents. All the recipe names in this book are in Sardo.

Sardo has three language "families"—Nuorese (east and inland, where I am from), Logoudorese (in the north and west), and Campidanese (in the south)—and within these families a total of more than sixty dialects (which is why Italian, not Sardo, is taught in schools). Thus you will find Sardo spoken everywhere; it just varies from home to home, town to town.

Sardinian shepherd's soup
Suppa de su Pastore
SERVES 4

Fregula kin Arsellas is Sardinia's signature soup of the sea. Suppa de su Pastore is our signature soup of the land. This classic shepherd's soup is simple and hearty but not heavy—representing our cuisine at its most rustic and fundamental. When people say Sardinian food has a rich tradition that developed from poor origins, they might have this dish in mind. The ingredients—lamb broth, young and aged pecorino, pane carasau—have been used by shepherds for centuries. And why not? The broth, cheese, bread, and mint are fantastic together. I remember having it the first time at a festival in the countryside, where it is customarily served after holiday meals and celebrations. Just don't show this version of the recipe to my mother. She considers it sacrilege to break a sheet of pane carasau to make the soup. She would make it only at the end of the month when odd shaped pieces remained in the bottom of the breadbasket.

◇　◇　◇

Bring broth to a slow boil. Break pane carasau sheets into many small pieces (about 2 to 4 inches in size).

Divide pane carasau among four bowls. Top each with pecorino cheese and mint.

Carefully pour broth into the bowls. Add shavings of the young pecorino cheese and a drizzling of extra virgin olive oil.

6 cups lamb broth (see following recipe on page 71) (or beef or vegetable stock)
4 whole sheets pane carasau (see page 22)
1 cup Pecorino Sardo cheese (or other pecorino cheese), finely grated
4 sprigs mint, finely chopped
¼ cup coarsely grated young mild Pecorino Sardo cheese (or other young pecorino cheese)
Extra virgin olive oil for drizzling

Lamb broth
Brou de Beccu
MAKES 4 CUPS

In Sardinia, where sheep outnumber people three to one, no shepherd's soup would be made from anything but a rich, meaty ram's broth. Don't discard the meat after you filter the stock. Sprinkle it with some fruttato olive oil and sea salt, accompany it with some good bread, and you have the makings of an excellent supper.

◇ ◇ ◇

Add the ram, vegetables, herbs, and salt to a large 8-quart stock pot. Add water to cover (about 8 cups), leaving room for liquid to boil. Boil for 10 minutes, occasionally skimming the top with a spoon to remove fat and impurities.

Reduce heat to low. Cover, with lid slightly askew, and cook for 3 hours. Remove from heat and let rest 30 minutes. Filter by passing through a sieve lined with cheesecloth.

2 pounds young ram (preferably shoulder meat)

1 medium carrot, cut into 2- to 3-inch pieces

1 medium white onion, quartered

1 Roma tomato, halved

1 bunch flat leaf parsley, coarsely chopped

1 bunch basil, coarsely chopped

1 bay leaf

1 teaspoon sea salt

ROTTEN CHEESE

There is one pecorino you would never use in this dish: *casu marzu* ("rotten cheese" in Sardo). Casu marzu is literally decomposing and alive with maggots that jump inches in the air when disturbed. The maggots create a rich, very soft, creamy (if somewhat runny) Sardinian delicacy that is both subtle and pungent.

Today, I cannot resist its charms, but as a child, I would stay clear of the table when the casu marzu came out. I remember first seeing it at the end of a baptism or wedding, when only the heart of the family remained. My grandfather would pull out a special wine and then a piece of cheese with holes filled with tiny clear maggots. I tried casu marzu for the first time when I was twelve. I was with a friend from a shepherd family; he dipped his fingers straight into it.

Don't expect to see casu marzu advertised at a local cheese shop in Sardinia: it is officially banned in Italy (largely because the maggots can live on in human intestines and cause some damage—though I have never seen anyone fall ill from it). In addition, only a few people still make this delicacy—usually for family and friends and, maybe, that local cheese shop that has hidden it under the counter.

Filindeu pasta in lamb broth
Filindeu kin Casu Friscu
SERVES 4

This soup is one of the rarest and most revered in Sardinia because of the filindeu: handmade threads of fresh angel hair pasta delicately woven into a "net" and then dried. (Filindeu loosely translates to "threads of God.") The pasta is so delicate it is served only in a soup. It is so difficult to make that just one woman in all of Sardinia still makes it by hand. She lives in Nuoro, the heart of inland Sardinia, where the soup is served every May at the Feast of Saint Francis. Held at the Church of Saint Francis in Lula, the feast is attended by pilgrims from all over Sardinia, who are given a bowl of this soup to welcome them after their journey. Elsewhere, it can be hard to find. When you do come across it, it is often served between lunch and dinner at a wedding or other celebration. I was honored to serve it at my son Valerio's baptism (pictured below). Filindeu aside, the ingredients are similar to suppa de su pastore but this version is thickened with pecorino.

◈　　◈　　◈

In a large pot, bring lamb broth to a boil. Add filindeu and cook for 3 minutes. Reduce heat and add the pecorino; stir gently and cheese will begin to melt, thickening the broth.

When cheese is incorporated, remove from heat. Stir in mint and drizzle with fruttato olive oil before serving.

4 cups lamb broth (see recipe, page 71)
5 ounces filindeu pasta, slightly broken (or angel hair pasta "nests")
¼ pound young Pecorino Sardo cheese (or other young pecorino cheese), shredded
4 sprigs fresh mint, torn
2 tablespoons fruttato extra virgin olive oil (see page 40)

Lentil soup with fregula and chicory
Fregula Lentizza e Zicoria

SERVES 4

Lentils, along with saffron, came to Sardinia with Arab invaders. I remember seeing bags of lentils stacked in the back room where Mannoi Loi kept them ready for soups or stews. Today, no one grows them in my town, and they are disappearing across the island—a tradition lost to time. Perhaps it is their association with our "poor" origins or the fact that local stores carry lentils from other places in the Mediterranean that explains their disappearance. For me, this humble recipe evokes a deeper connection to the land that I grew up with—a connection I hope Sardinians will reclaim and preserve with our other ancient ingredients that are disappearing.

◇　◇　◇

Soak dried lentils in fresh water overnight (at least 8 hours). Drain before using.

In a large stock pot, heat olive oil and pancetta over medium heat. Cook until fat is rendered. Add garlic and chicory and cook for 5 minutes.

Stir in lentils, mixing well for flavors to combine. Pour vegetable stock into pot and bring to a boil. Cook for 5 minutes. Season with salt to taste. Add fregula and cook for 10 minutes. Remove from heat and stir in the fruttato olive oil. Serve sprinkled with ricotta salata.

1 cup green lentils

2 tablespoons extra virgin olive oil

2 ounces pancetta, chopped

2 garlic cloves, thinly sliced

1 cup chopped chicory

Sea salt

6 cups vegetable stock

1¼ cups fregula (see page 119)

4 tablespoons fruttato extra virgin olive oil
   (see page 40)

2 to 3 ounces ricotta salata cheese, grated

RICOTTA AND RICOTTA SALATA

As you would imagine, our nation of shepherds produces incredible fresh *recottu*, or ricotta in Italian. The name means "re-cooked" and refers to the cheese made from what is left in the pot after removing the cooked curd. As it cooks, the cheese looks like snowflakes as it rises bright white against the sides of the shepherd's copper pot. If you are lucky enough to be with the shepherd at that moment, there is little that is more wonderful to eat on a piece of pane carasau than that warm, creamy ricotta. The ricotta is then placed in baskets and drained to make the fresh ricotta (*ricotta gentile*) we use to fill ravioli, to finish soups, or to make sauces for pasta. It is also used to fill our sweet ravioli and pastries for dessert or served alone, sweetened with some bitter honey or abbamele.

While most Americans know fresh ricotta, these days you can also find ricotta salata in most cheese shops and gourmet grocers. Ricotta salata is simply fresh ricotta that is pressed into wheels, cured in brine (*salata* means "salted" in Italian), dried, and then aged for a few days or up to a month. The result is a hard, white cheese that is terrific for shaving or grating over soups, salads, pastas, and other dishes or served alone on a cheese plate.

Grilled lamb sweetbreads with blackberries
Carresapida de Anzone Arrustu

SERVES 4

Twice a year the shepherds brought baby lambs to Orosei for the slaughter—once at the start of spring and again for Christmas. Zio Valerio was one of the few locals contracted to butcher them. This was a special honor, reflecting the skill my uncle honed year after year as he expertly skinned the animals and processed their tender meat. Great ritual surrounded the slaughter. The shepherds gathered the lambs in the fields north of town, and the butchers did not stop working until the day was done. In the evening, the shepherds rewarded the butchers with the sweetbreads (thymus gland) and cordedda (intestines, see page 182) of the lambs. My uncle took home the cordedda, but he threw the sweetbreads on the fire, eating them right there with a little salt and pane carasau and a glass of new wine. They were gone in minutes—so quickly that if you walked away, you missed your chance. I got to join him one time and was amazed by the flavor of the grilled sweetbreads. If you have only had sweetbreads fried or sautéed, you must try them grilled. After tasting the smoky, charred tenderness, you will immediately understand why walking away from the fire was a bad idea.

◇　　◇　　◇

Season sweetbreads with salt and pepper. Place directly on a preheated grill. Cook 8 to 10 minutes, turning once.

Cut cooked sweetbreads into strips and place on a bed of mixed greens.

In a small bowl, mix olive oil and red wine vinegar. Drizzle vinaigrette over the sweetbreads and sprinkle with salt to taste. Top with blackberries.

1 pound baby lamb (or veal) sweetbreads, trimmed
Sea salt and freshly ground black pepper
8 cups field greens
⅓ cup extra virgin olive oil
2 tablespoons red wine vinegar
1 cup blackberries (preferably wild)

Roasted cheese with pane carasau
and bitter honey
Pane kin Casu Arrustu
SERVES 4

In Sardinia, this recipe is often prepared and served at the end of the meal next to the fireplace. In my house, it was best when Zio Gavino brought over his finest cheese and roasted it on the coals by our fire, turning and scraping the melted cheese directly onto the bread and leaving the rest by the fire as we ate. The jar of bitter honey would sit near the flames, too—how we all fought to lick that spoon! Today, when my children ask my mother for a snack, this is what she makes for them. This recipe goes in the oven if you don't have a fireplace, but the cheese can also be cooked on foil directly on a grill.

⬧　⬧　⬧

Toast bread lightly with a drizzling of extra virgin olive oil.

Preheat oven to 350°F. Place cheese on a baking sheet lined with parchment paper. Bake for 5 minutes; finish by placing under the broiler for 2 minutes for top to brown.

Warm bitter honey until easily drizzled. Scrape the melted cheese onto the toasted bread. Drizzle with warm bitter honey.

2 slices of pane carasau (see page 22), or
    8 pieces hard-crusted bread
Extra virgin olive oil for drizzling
8 wedges young, mild Pecorino Sardo cheese
    (or other pecorino cheese), about ¼ inch
    thick
3 to 4 tablespoons bitter honey (see
    page 229)

Marinated sea bass with lobster tail and bottarga
Carpaccio de Ispigola kin Aligusta
SERVES 4

Sardinians, *whose fishermen know no greater delicacy than sea urchin cracked open and eaten immediately with a splash of lemon, have no issues with raw fish. So why does my father, when I serve him this recipe, say "Go. Go back to America." It is not as if this is an American dish. Its ingredients are found in countless Sardinian recipes. Some of his resistance probably has to do with the lingering Sardinian suspicion of the sea, but mostly it is because this dish caters to the more modern tastes of the island and its visitors. Simply put, this is not a dish my father grew up eating. Today, seafood carpaccios are fixtures on menus in Arbatax, Cagliari, and La Costa Smeralda. Even Zia Maria serves them at my family's inn, Su Barchile, but only in the summer when "outsiders" visit. If you enjoy ceviche or sushi, you will love this dish.*

⬧　⬧　⬧

Slice sea bass into thin slices about ¼ inch each. Lay slices between sheets of plastic wrap that have been lightly moistened with water. Pound until paper-thin with a mallet or meat pounder (even a rolling pin works well). Spread sea bass in one layer on baking sheets with ½-inch sides.

In a small bowl, combine saffron, chives, lemon zest, lime zest, salt, and pepper. Sprinkle dry mix on the fish. In another bowl, combine lemon juice, lime juice, and ¼ cup of the olive oil and drizzle on fish. Brush or rub to coat evenly.

Cover with plastic wrap pressed directly onto the fish. Make sure no air pockets are between the plastic wrap and fish. Place in refrigerator to marinate at least 4 hours.

Boil lobster tail in salted water just until cooked through, about 7 minutes. Transfer to a bowl of ice water to cool and stop the cooking process. Remove meat from tail and cut into medallions.

Layer the sea bass on the serving plate, reserving the marinade. Top with greens and lobster medallions. Top with shavings of bottarga and drizzle with reserved marinade and remaining ¼ cup olive oil.

½ pound sea bass fillet, skinned and deboned
¼ teaspoon saffron, crushed into powder
¼ cup minced chives
Juice and grated zest of 1 lemon
Juice and grated zest of 2 limes
¼ teaspoon sea salt
⅛ teaspoon freshly ground black pepper
½ cup extra virgin olive oil
1 lobster tail (about 8 ounces)
¼ pound baby greens
4 ounces bottarga di muggine (see page 30), thinly shaved

LA COSTA SMERALDA

Until recently, if people in the United States knew anything about Sardinia, they knew about La Costa Smeralda, or the Emerald Coast. Once a desolate shoreline between Porto Cervo and Porto Rotondo in the northern Gallura region, the Emerald Coast has been transformed over the past forty years into a playground for the rich and famous, with luxury resorts and magnificent homes dotting the coastline. Much of the development is the vision of an international magnate, Prince Karim Aga Khan. Today there is no place more exclusive or more expensive in all of Italy.

The Emerald Coast does not represent the traditional side of Sardinia, but its success did the rest of us a wealth of good: it brought Sardinia international exposure; awoke us to the potential for tourism; and forced us to restrict further development along the coastline to maintain the beaches, cliffs, and rivers. It also opened up the culinary landscape, allowing for more sophisticated creations using traditional ingredients.

Marinated tomato and swordfish with baby greens and capers
Carpaccio de Piske Ispada kin Capperos

SERVES 4

Our seafaring tradition may be young compared to Sicily's, but from lobstermen in Alghero to the tuna fishermen of Carloforte and Olbia, we are learning fast. The ancient city of Cagliari in the south, the glamorous Gallura region in the north, the spectacular rocce rosse (red cliffs) of Arbatax in the east, the dunes of Oristano in the west–our finest fishermen fill these ports with the best the Mediterranean has to offer. As a result, you now find more deepwater fish like swordfish in Sardinia. Of course, most Sardinians still follow my father's decree for cooking it: fire, olive oil, and salt. In time that will likely change. I have always felt swordfish has an appealing sweetness and fatty texture that can be missed when you cook it. So I thought again of a carpaccio using capers, which are very common in the south of Sardinia. A few more ingredients than the older generation would like perhaps, but still in the spirit of the old recipes, in which the ingredients do not hide the flavor of the fish but enhance it–making it stronger and more intense.

◇　◇　◇

In a small bowl, combine ½ cup of the olive oil and the lemon juice. Lightly brush some of the marinade on the bottom of a baking sheet with ½-inch sides.

Cut the swordfish into ¼-inch slices. Lay slices between sheets of plastic wrap that have been lightly moistened with water. Pound to a paper-thin thickness with a mallet or meat pounder (even a rolling pin works well). Lay swordfish on baking sheet and brush evenly with remaining marinade.

Cover with plastic wrap pressed directly onto the fish. Make sure no air pockets are between the plastic wrap and fish. Place in refrigerator to marinate at least 2 hours.

Place layers of tomatoes on the serving plate. Top with the marinated swordfish. Mound greens in the center and sprinkle with the capers.

Combine lime juice and mosto d'uva. Add remaining olive oil. Drizzle on the plate and season with salt and pepper to taste. Sprinkle with the chopped basil.

½ cup plus 2 tablespoons single-orchard
　　extra virgin olive oil (see page 40)
Juice of 1 lemon
1 swordfish fillet (about 12 ounces)
2 large beefsteak tomatoes, cut into paper-
　　thin slices
¼ pound baby greens
½ cup capers, drained
1 tablespoon lime juice
1 tablespoon mosto d'uva (see page 42)
2 sprigs basil, chopped
Sea salt and freshly ground black pepper

Pan-seared scallops with fregula and roasted vegetables
Capesante kin Fregula e Taffaranu
SERVES 4

I do a lot of cooking classes and demonstrations of Sardinian ingredients and cuisine across America. At these events, I often get the chance to do just one recipe that is supposed to "take" people to Sardinia. This is a difficult job for me: thousands of years of history, dozens of indigenous ingredients, countless stories, but only a few hours and one or two recipes. I created this dish for those situations. The mix of traditional ingredients, the color of the vegetables, and the sear on the scallops make a beautiful presentation. But it is the sweet drizzle of abbamele that really "transports" this dish, enhancing the mild flavor of the scallops and fregula and balancing the peppery arugula. I always try to serve it with a glass of another Sardinian culinary staple: Vermentino di Gallura (see page 130).

◇   ◇   ◇

In a medium saucepan, bring 1 cup chicken stock to a boil. Add fregula, bay leaf, saffron, 1 tablespoon of olive oil, and a pinch of sea salt; cook, covered, for 8 to 10 minutes. All liquid should be absorbed by the fregula.

Heat 2 tablespoons olive oil in a medium skillet over medium heat. Sauté green onions, shallot, and celery for 2 to 3 minutes. Add zucchini, squash, and tomato and cook for 2 to 3 minutes. Combine fregula and vegetables and cook on low heat for another minute. Add additional stock or hot water if mixture is dry.

In a medium nonstick skillet, heat remaining 2 tablespoons olive oil. Cook scallops until golden and sprinkle with a pinch of sea salt. Turn and brown other side.

Divide fregula mixture among four plates and top with finely chopped arugula. Top each with three scallops. Finish with a drizzling of warm abbamele and olive oil.

1 cup chicken stock, plus more if needed
1 cup fregula (see page 119)
1 bay leaf
1 pinch saffron
5 tablespoons extra virgin olive oil, plus more for drizzling
2 pinches sea salt
2 green onions, chopped
1 shallot, chopped
1 stalk celery, diced
1 zucchini (preferably with blossom), diced
1 yellow squash, diced
1 Roma tomato, seeded and diced
12 diver sea scallops (note—if using smaller scallops, increase quantity)
1 bunch arugula, finely chopped (about ½ cup)
1 tablespoon abbamele (see page 59), warm

Sardinian cheeses, cured meats, delicacies from the sea
Assazos de Casu | Affitatu de Issacatos e Pressuttu | Crudos de Mare

*P*latters of cheese, cured meat, or shellfish are fundamental parts of the Sardinian table and culture. Cheese and meat have ancient origins in Sardinia and are common in homes across the island. A shepherd might offer them for lunch at his house with some pane carasau to use as a plate or to moisten and roll with prosciutto and a piece of pecorino. All accompanied, of course, by a glass of the shepherd's red wine pulled from a dark corner where he keeps it waiting for just this moment.

At the shepherd's house, cheese and meat would be served on an avaione (a cork plate, see page 212) garnished with mirto (myrtle) or corbezzolo (strawberry tree) branches. Other homes might have trays made from wild olive or pear trees. The meats will be thinly sliced and the cheese cut from large pieces at the table (sometimes from a quarter or half wheel). Shellfish would be served in a ceramic bowl or on a metal tray on a bed of crushed ice, the treasures of the sea piled on top, with wedges of lemon on the side.

Cheese

For many Sardinians, including myself, cheese is the soul of these platters. The importance of pecorino to Sardinia cannot be overstated: yesterday ends and today begins with cheese; it can come out at any time except when you are sleeping (see page 27 for more on pecorino). A meal seldom ends without pecorino—it cleanses the palate and returns you to the red wine and conversation.

The oldest and most important among these pecorinos are Fiore Sardo ("Flower of Sardinia") and Pecorino Sardo. Both are classified DOP (Denominazióne di Origine Protetta)—a tightly monitored European Union label that guarantees the production is high quality and Sardinian-only. Pecorino Sardo can range from mild and young (aged twenty to sixty days) to sharp and mature (aged a year or more). Fiore Sardo production is one of the most ancient cheese traditions on the island and still uses the original shepherd techniques to curdle the whole sheep's milk with baby lamb or even goat stomach (rennet). Firm in texture with a straw or white color, it has a lightly smoked and rich flavor that can be mild (three months) or sharp (six months).

I love to present guests with selections in addition to Fiore Sardo and Pecorino Sardo, from these other Sardinian cheeses at the end of a meal, and I recommend the same to you: caprino (soft, creamy whole milk goat cheese—also great for a light breakfast with a little bitter honey), casizzolu (full cream from milk of the "red cow," see pages 135 and 172), ricotta fresca (delicate and fresh, made from sheep's milk whey), and pecorino semi-stagionato (a three- to six-month old pecorino).

Cured Meats

When I am lucky enough to visit my friend Gianni's cucina rustica in Berchidda and get some of his hanging guanciale (unsmoked bacon from pig's jowels or cheeks) or salsicce (seasoned sausage from lean and fatty pigs studded with fennel seeds and herbs; it looks like a donut when cured), the moment stays with me for days. Not everyone can cure meat like Gianni (who, like most Sardinians, cures meat mostly from pigs), but everyone has a little cured meat "hanging around" to cook with or offer a guest. The quality of Sardinian cured meat is so high, rumor has it that the Vatican buys Sardinian salsicce. In addition, my other favorites include: capocollo (exceptionally high quality cured meat from pig shoulder), guanciale, lardo (cured lard), pancetta (salt-cured pork belly), prosciutto (either *di pecora*, from sheep, or *di Desulo*, from the leg or shoulders of free-range pigs), and salami cut from pig legs (same as salsicce but bigger, with a casing made from large intestines).

Shellfish

When I visit port towns like Olbia, Alghero, and even Orosei, where fisherman offer quality shellfish that can be eaten raw, I indulge in these Sardinian fruits of the sea. Not all are easy to find, but when I do see them, they make my mouth water. I especially cannot resist the explosion of flavors in every bite of *orticata* (sea anemone). If I am going to be in Orosei in the fall, I will call Zia Maria at Su Barchile, our family's inn, and ask her to set aside some for me. Or I will head to La Marina when the fishermen return with their bounty. But summer is the peak time for these other Sardinian shellfish delicacies: *arsellas* and *tartufi di mare* (clams), *bocconi* (sea snails or whelks), *cozzas* (mussels), *ostriche* (oysters), *pattelle* (limpids), and *ovos de erithu* (sea urchin). You will find more about many of them in recipes throughout this book.

Assembly Required

Fiore Sardo and Pecorino Sardo are available in the United States, but substitutions for the fresh cheeses not available can be found in cheese shops and farmers' markets. Versions of all the cured meats and suitable shellfish substitutions are available in the United States, though some are harder to find than others. I did not, however, include the wild boar and lamb prosciutto I love–you will have to go to Sardinia for those. Remember to take the cheeses and meats out of the refrigerator about an hour before serving time, since they reach their optimal texture and flavor at room temperature.

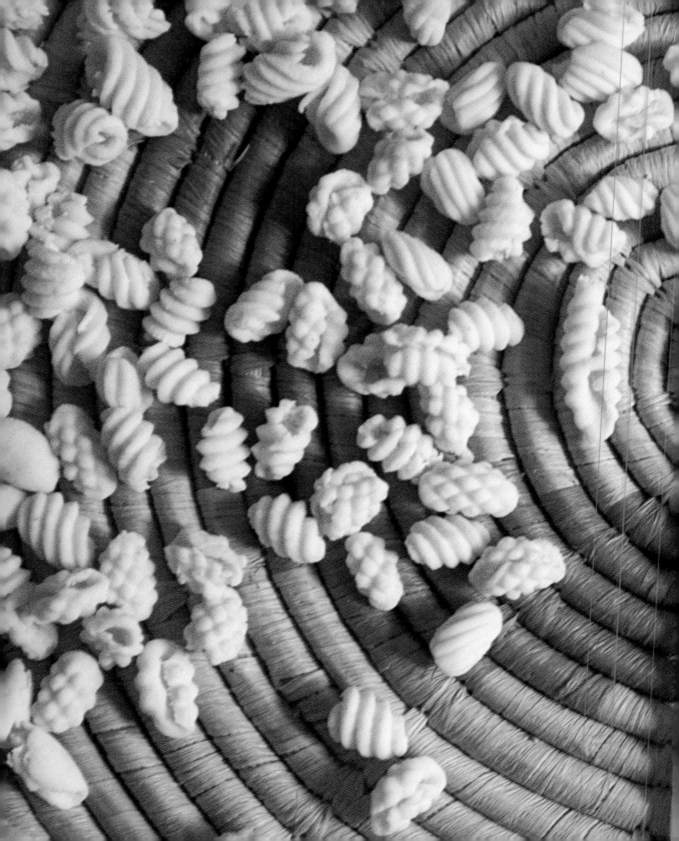

Pastas & Risottos
Macarrones

◇

Chie juchet urchetta, mandicat macarrones.

"Whoever has a fork, can eat pasta."

Even after decades in America, I am always surprised to hear someone say, "I want spaghetti for dinner." We never did. My mother did not wake up and say, "Today we will have spaghetti with tomato sauce." She said, "Today we will have macarrones." Then, the *sauce* she made determined what shape pasta (macarrones) she would use. After all, pasta is always made from the same basic ingredients–flour, egg, water–and the shape you choose is only a vessel for the sauce. The sauce was like a mood–what do we feel like today? (and what could we afford?)–and the shape balanced that mood. We had many moods and macarrones to choose from. Pasta is everywhere in Sardinia and many of the shapes will be familiar: spaghetti, fettuccini, ravioli, and penne have been made on the island for centuries, as have risottos, which are included here. But a few of our signature macarrones–fregula, malloreddus, macarrones de busa–are not widely known–yet. But whichever you use, just try and think about the sauce first.

Pasta to celebrate the harvest of the grain
Macarrones de Ariola
SERVES 4

Mannoi Arre used to tell me that harvesting wheat and hauling it to the Ariola for separating was brutal work. Under a hot sun, fifteen to twenty men cut the wheat stalks by hand, working at a brisk pace. Even in the heat, they wore scarves around their necks to protect their skin and keep out the dust, especially when the wind blew the tops of the wheat everywhere. With only a barrel of warm water under a tree to quench their thirst and the shade of one tree to cool them, they had no time to stop for mere exhaustion. When the men were at their most hungry and tired, a beautiful site appeared along the horizon: a line of six to ten women—mothers, daughters, sisters—marching toward them, black skirts and white shirts in stark contrast to the sky. The men called them "sas corallinas" (a "beautiful sight" like coral). On her head, each woman carried a ceramic pot wrapped in cloth, steam escaping from the top. The pot held this pasta dish made with tomato sauce and young and aged pecorino cheese. The dish finished cooking in the long walk to the field. Nothing was more refreshing or welcome. The pasta was wonderful, too.

◇　◇　◇

Heat the tomato sauce to a gentle boil in a medium saucepan.

Bring a large pot of salted water to a boil, add pasta and boil for 10 to 12 minutes, or until al dente. Drain. Combine the cheeses in a small bowl.

In a ceramic serving dish, assemble by alternating layers of tomato sauce, cheese, and pasta to create at least three layers. Top generously with tomato sauce and cheese to finish. Cover with a lid or aluminum foil.

Wrap dish with a towel to insulate heat and let it set for 30 minutes before serving. To serve, scoop with a serving spoon through all the layers.

Note: When cooking the pasta, give it a few extra minutes beyond al dente. This will help it set better and allow serving through the layers.

4 cups tomato sauce (see recipe page 92)

1 pound bucatini pasta

1 cup grated Pecorino Sardo cheese (aged about 2 years) (or other aged pecorino cheese)

1 cup grated Pecorino Sardo cheese (aged about 8 months) (or other young pecorino cheese)

THE ARIOLA

Every family in Orosei had 10 acres north of town given to them by the government to raise grain. The men built small shelters there, because they often left for days at a time to work the soil, plant the seeds, tend to the crop, and finally harvest the wheat. After harvesting, my family brought the wheat to the ariola, a large open field where families and farmers prepared their products for home or market. It was the place where everyone gathered after the harvest. My family loaded their carts with stalks of wheat from their fields and took them there to separate the tops of the wheat by hand. There an ox turned a giant stone wheel that separated the wheat. When they returned home, the women would clean and store the grain we used for bread and pasta for the year.

My mother's tomato sauce
Bagna de Mamma

YIELDS 4 CUPS

When tomatoes filled our gardens in the summer and early fall, my mother's mornings often went something like this: make the morning coffee; start making tomato sauce. She chopped the onions, garlic, and her special amount of carrots and celery. She went to the garden to cut fresh basil. Maybe she threw in a pork bone or a piece of meat she had saved for the sauce. While the garlic heated on the stove, she strained the tomatoes through her food mill. The sauce then simmered all morning. The smell in our kitchen was enchanting and so was watching my mother (pictured at right with my grandmother, seated).

◇ ◇ ◇

Heat olive oil, garlic, and bay leaf in a large saucepan over medium heat. In a bowl, crush canned tomatoes with a food mill or a fork, discarding any unripened pieces, and add with juices to saucepan. Add celery, carrot, green onion, and basil.

Bring the mixture to a boil. Reduce the heat to medium-low and let the sauce simmer for 25 minutes, stirring frequently to prevent sticking. Remove the bay leaf, carrot, and celery before using the sauce.

½ cup extra virgin olive oil

1 garlic clove, chopped

1 bay leaf

3 cans (14.5 ounce) peeled plum tomatoes, undrained (or 4 pounds Roma tomatoes, seeded and chopped)

1 celery stalk, halved

1 medium carrot, halved

1 extra large green onion, chopped

2 sprigs basil, chopped

PEELING TOMATOES

You will notice that some of the recipes in this book call for tomatoes to be peeled, seeded, and diced. So it is fair to ask: Did my mother do it this way? The answer is yes. If my mother did not want seeds or skin, she took the time to take them out. When she preserved tomatoes for the winter to use for this sauce, she peeled, cooked, seeded, and ground them in a food mill before she filled the jars.

The rustic origin of Sardinian cuisine may be synonymous with simple combinations and straightforward preparations, but it is not synonymous with quick or easy. This is not fast food; cooking took all day. My mother and the women of my family took pride in everything they did; they took the time to make the home look—and the food taste—the way they wanted it to. But of course, unlike most home cooks today in the United States, my mother never threw away the parts she did not use: the animals or the garden, not the garbage can, got the seeds and skin.

Pasta for Good Friday
Malloreddus de Kita Santa

SERVES 4

Sardinia is a devout nation, as you can tell from our worship of the saints, the magnitude of Carnevale (see the desserts chapter), and the importance of holidays like Easter. Thus, one of the few times Sardinians will willingly go without meat for any extended period of time is Lent, and no one eats meat on Friday, especially Kita Santa or Good Friday. This is my version of a traditional vegetarian pasta dish we serve on that day. I love the mixture of rosemary, basil, walnuts, bread crumbs, cheese, and pasta so much that I might eat this dish on Good Friday even if meat were permitted.

◊　◊　◊

Bring a large pot of salted water to a boil, add the malloreddus and boil for 10 to 12 minutes, or until al dente.

Heat the olive oil in a saucepan over medium heat. Add garlic and cook until softened. Add pasta and toss.

In a small bowl, mix basil, rosemary, parsley, and walnuts. Add the mixture to the pasta and toss to combine. Stir in bread crumbs and butter. Mix well.

Before serving, stir in the pecorino cheese.

1 pound malloreddus pasta

¼ cup extra virgin olive oil

3 garlic cloves, finely chopped

4 sprigs basil, finely chopped

1 sprig rosemary, tender leaves finely chopped

¼ cup chopped flat leaf parsley

⅓ cup chopped walnuts

½ cup bread crumbs

2 tablespoons unsalted butter

½ cup grated Pecorino Sardo cheese (or other pecorino cheese)

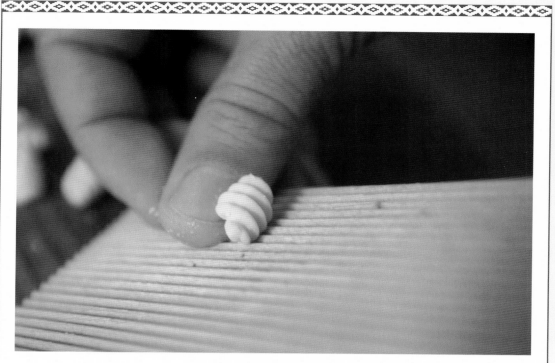

MALLOREDDUS

The first signature pasta in this chapter is actually the last shape created when making pasta. Growing up, all of the pasta in my home was handmade, and Zia Mary made most of it (see sidebar, page 113). She started with ravioli and fettuccini—those that required the most dough and surface space—and finished by making the teardrop-sized malloreddus from the last bits and trimmings of dough (nothing was ever wasted!). In fact, *malloreddus* means "calves" in Sardo, probably because they are "born" from the larger shapes. From the last ball of dough, little pieces no larger than a fingernail are pressed and rolled on the irregular surface of the table, a small ribbed board, or a piece of glass called a ciurili to create the pasta's distinctive ridges. The little dumplinglike shapes have an appealing chewiness that makes them ideal for a simple tomato sauce with grated aged pecorino cheese or rich meat ragùs or creamy sauces or even just a little olive oil and grated bottarga. They are sometimes packaged under their Italian name, gnocchetti sardi, and occasionally flavored with saffron.

Pasta with ricotta and bottarga
Macarrones kin Recottu

SERVES 4

You might have a creamy sauce like this one in any shepherd's home (perhaps made right in front of you in the same pot as the ricotta). When I make this dish at home, I like to indulge the sea in me and add bottarga; the combination is not traditional but honors my devotion to land and sea and enhances the flavor of all the ingredients. The thick sauce calls for short macarrones like malloreddus, because it coats the pasta inside and out and would weigh down any larger shapes.

◇　◇　◇

Bring a large pot of salted water to a boil, add malloreddus and boil for 10 to 12 minutes, or until al dente.

While cooking the pasta, heat the heavy cream in a large saucepan over medium heat. Add ricotta and stir well to combine. Cook for 5 minutes, continuously stirring until the sauce thickens and is well combined. Stir in 2 tablespoons of bottarga and freshly ground black pepper to taste.

Drain pasta and add to ricotta mixture. Add parsley and toss well to combine; stir in the olive oil. Pour pasta mixture into a ceramic serving dish, then sprinkle with the remaining 2 tablespoons of bottarga.

1 pound malloreddus pasta (or short tubular pasta) (see page 95)

1 cup heavy cream

1 cup sheep's milk ricotta cheese (or other creamy ricotta cheese)

4 tablespoons grated bottarga di muggine (see page 30)

Freshly ground black pepper

1 bunch flat leaf parsley, finely chopped

2 tablespoons extra virgin olive oil

Malloreddus with pork and pancetta
Malloreddus kin Purpuzza

SERVES 4

My happiest food memories surround events that brought the family together: baking pane carasau, making sweets for a wedding or Carnevale, and, of course, the killing of a pig. I describe this ritual through recipes starting on page 156, but to this day, any time I make this dish or smell pork meat or sausage browning, I am instantly transported to Mannoi Arre's house and the cucina rustica where we butchered the pig. When we were done cutting up the meat and making the sausage, there would be little bits of leftover meat and fat on the table. We scooped them up and sautéed them in the pan and then simmered them until tender to make this dish celebrating the end of the ritual. Since the pork meat available today is so lean, I have added a little pancetta to the ingredients in this recipe.

◇　◇　◇

Place the pork and pancetta in a large bowl. With a mortar and pestle, mash garlic and pepper into a paste. Mix in the vinegar. Toss pork and marinade until mixed well. Cover and refrigerate for 4 hours.

In a skillet over medium-high heat, brown the pork and pancetta for 5 minutes. Add the red wine and deglaze, scraping browned bits from bottom of pan.

Add sun-dried tomatoes, tomato paste, and myrtle leaves to skillet. Add chicken stock, cover, and simmer for 30 minutes.

Bring a large pot of salted water to a boil. Add malloreddus and boil for 10 to 12 minutes, or until al dente. Remove myrtle from sauce and discard. Toss pasta with sauce. Sprinkle with pecorino cheese and finish with a drizzling of olive oil.

1 pound pork shoulder, cut into ½-inch cubes

¼ pound pancetta, ½-inch slices, cut into cubes

½ garlic clove

1 pinch freshly ground black pepper

2 teaspoons red wine vinegar

½ cup Terra Saliosa wine (or other dry red wine)

¼ cup sun-dried tomatoes, chopped

1 tablespoon tomato paste

1 sprig myrtle (see page 231), about 5 to 6 leaves

1½ cups chicken stock

1 pound malloreddus pasta (see page 95)

½ cup grated Pecorino Sardo cheese (or other pecorino cheese)

2 tablespoons single-orchard extra virgin olive oil (see page 40)

CUCINA RUSTICA

Cucina rustica translates to "rustic kitchen," but that translation does not exactly describe this space in the traditional Sardinian home. First of all, the cucina rustica was not a room per se but an area in the back of the house, partially covered, and opening onto a courtyard. It had a fireplace and a table, and we used it for everything from butchering a pig to making pasta. The floor was made of a beautiful stone or tile that had been packed into the earth from decades, even centuries, of use. Today many old Sardinian homes, like my grandfather's house (where Zia Mary now lives) or my sister and brother-in-law's house in the old city of Nuoro, still have a cucina rustica, but the spaces have been converted into large dining rooms or work areas. Some have committed the sin of modernizing with linoleum floors and Formica counters. But many, like my sister Angela's (pictured above), are particularly beautiful with a large fireplace to cook in and a long table that seats twenty people comfortably. They remain a place for cooking and gathering around the table.

Malloreddus from the Baronia
Malloreddus a sa Baroniesa

SERVES 4

Sardinia is a nation of regions: Barbagia, Gallura, Logudoro, Campidano. Orosei and the surrounding towns are part of the Baronia, named for the barons who ruled the area centuries ago. This regional recipe of the Baronia is a spring favorite of ours. It originates not from the homes of the barons, but those of the "common people" who, along with the clergy, made up the three classifications of people in the region. Prepared with new potatoes, bacon, and supersweet and juicy green onions, the texture and flavor of this spicy dish are in stark contrast to a ragù. It is also is easier to make and takes much less time.

◇ ◇ ◇

Rinse and clean new potatoes well, checking cavities for soil. Boil potatoes in salted water for 20 minutes until tender. Transfer potatoes to a bowl filled with ice water to stop the cooking process. Drain well. Leaving skin on, cut potatoes into ¼-inch sticks; set aside.

Heat olive oil in a medium saucepan over medium heat. Add onion, pancetta, and pepperoncino. Cook until pancetta is browned, being careful not to burn.

Add potatoes and salt to taste, then incorporate the wine, cooking until absorbed. Cover and set aside, keeping warm.

Cook pasta in salted boiling water for 10 to 12 minutes, or until al dente. Drain pasta and add to the sauce. Toss well to combine. Return to heat and cook for 2 minutes to combine flavors.

Stir in parsley and pecorino cheese before serving.

1 pound new potatoes

¼ cup extra virgin olive oil

1 medium onion, sliced

4 ounces pancetta, thinly sliced, chopped into 1-inch pieces

1 whole fresh pepperoncino, halved (or ½ to 1 teaspoon crushed red pepper)

Sea salt

1 cup Vermentino wine (or other dry white wine)

1 pound malloreddus pasta (see page 95)

½ bunch flat leaf parsley, finely chopped

½ cup grated Pecorino Sardo cheese (or other pecorino cheese)

THE BARONIA

The Baronia region (of which Orosei is a part) was named after the barons in the Kingdom of Sardinia who ruled the area from the Middle Ages through The War of the Spanish Succession in the eighteenth century. The Baronia also plays an important part in our literary history as the setting for Grazia Deledda's 1913 novel *Reeds in the Wind* (*Canne al Vento*). Born in Nuoro, Deledda is Sardinia's greatest writer and in 1926 became the second woman—and first Italian and only Sardinian—to win the Nobel Prize in Literature. By the time she died in 1936, she had written 33 novels and dozens of short stories. *Reeds in the Wind* is one of her finest novels, a sweeping tale of the Pintor sisters and the rise and fall of their aristocratic family. ("We are reeds, and fate is the wind.") The story starts in the present with the sisters struggling to survive in their rundown home and tells their history through flashbacks. This dish with its potatoes, bacon, and green onions is exactly the kind of humble dish the sisters' wise and loyal servant Efix might have eaten.

Malloreddus with lamb ragù and lamb chops
Malloreddus kin Anzone

SERVES 4

I learned to make ragùs from sausage or the bits of meat and fat leftover from the butchering of the animals—the scraps and tougher shoulder meat from pig, wild boar, and lamb. This recipe honors the ragù technique I learned from my mother and offers a great way to get more out of your modern rack of lamb. Instead of just throwing away the wonderful trimmings (which is quite hard on my Sardinian conscience), use them in this hearty dish. I say "modern" rack of lamb, because rack of lamb and lamb chops, so common in today's meat counters, were not cuts our butchers made in Sardinia. My mother would walk into a butcher shop and say, "I'm making dinner for my family, give me four pounds." Then she would specify where she wanted it cut from—in this case shoulder meat for a ragù. She would simmer it with her tomato sauce just as I have here. The addition of the lamb chops makes it a complete and filling meal—a real stick-to-your-bones winter dish. Note: Make sure you check that there is extra meat on the rack of lamb. If there is not a lot of meat, pick up some cubed shoulder meat as well and add it to the recipe.

◈ ◈ ◈

If using lamb chops and shoulder meat, chop the meat into small cubes and set aside.

If using a rack of lamb: Clean the rack of lamb, trimming the fat and reserving the meat. Make sure when you trim the fat from the lamb that you preserve the meat. Do not worry about precision—if there is extra fat on the lamb, it will reduce when you make the ragù. Chop the meat into small cubes and set aside. Divide the rack into the eight chops.

In a medium saucepan, heat the olive oil, shallots, thyme, and rosemary over medium heat. Sear the chops on each side. Set aside.

Add the chopped meat to the saucepan and simmer for 2 minutes. Season with salt and pepper to taste. Add the bay leaf and onion. Simmer for 5 minutes, until meat has browned.

Add wine, stirring frequently, and deglaze, scraping browned bits from bottom of the pan. Add tomato sauce and basil. Let simmer on low heat for 15 minutes. (Add lamb or vegetable stock if sauce becomes dry.)

Return lamb chops to the saucepan and cook for another 15 minutes until the lamb cubes are tender. Remove chops and set aside, keeping warm.

Bring a large pot of salted water to a boil, add malloreddus and cook for 10 to 12 minutes, until al dente. Drain. Transfer the pasta to a bowl. Gently mix in the tomato and lamb sauce. Incorporate the pecorino into the pasta mixture. Top each serving with two lamb chops.

1 medium rack of lamb (with 8 chops) or 8 lamb chops, plus 1 pound shoulder meat

2 tablespoons extra virgin olive oil

2 shallots, quartered

Sea salt and freshly ground black pepper

1 sprig rosemary

2 sprigs thyme

1 bay leaf

1 small white onion, chopped

1 cup Cannonau wine (or other dry red wine)

2 cups tomato sauce (see recipe, page 92)

1 sprig fresh basil, chopped

1 pound malloreddus pasta (see page 95)

½ cup grated aged Pecorino Sardo cheese (or other pecorino cheese)

Pasta with lamb and fava beans
Macarrones kin Ava Frisca

SERVES 4

My mother's recipes always remind me of the importance of freshness and seasonality by showing how each season offers its own superb combination of flavors. Take lamb. Even beyond its association with Easter, lamb is our quintessential spring meat and combines with other spring ingredients like artichokes and new potatoes (see page 178) or, in this pasta dish, with fresh fava beans. My mother still makes this dish today, sometimes substituting green peas for the favas or some chunks of lamb shoulder for the leg (making it more like a stew). She pairs the sauce with orecchiette, a chewy shell-shaped pasta which looks like ears (orecchiette means "little ears" in Italian) made by pressing your thumb into a small piece of dough.

◇　◇　◇

Heat the olive oil in a saucepan over medium-high heat. Add leek, pearl onions, and rosemary and heat until onions soften. Add the lamb and cook until browned.

Deglaze the pan with the red wine. Add tomato puree, 1 cup water, and fava beans. Simmer for 15 minutes, until the beans are tender. Stir in the basil.

Bring large pot of salted water to a boil, add pasta and boil for for 12 to 15 minutes, until al dente. Drain. Add pasta to the sauce and toss well.

Stir in the pecorino cheese before serving.

¼ cup extra virgin olive oil

½ leek, white part only, finely julienned

12 pearl onions, halved

1 sprig rosemary, leaves chopped

½ pound lamb leg, trimmed and cut into ½-inch cubes

½ cup Cannonau wine (or other dry red wine)

1 cup tomato puree

1 cup shelled fresh fava beans

1 sprig basil, chopped

1 pound orecchiette pasta

½ cup grated Pecorino Sardo cheese (or other pecorino cheese)

Lamb ravioli with lamb ragù
Anzelottos de Petha

SERVES 4

Lamb and peas create a terrific filling and sauce for ravioli in this traditional spring recipe. It comes from my friend Pasquale's father, Giampiero; both live in the town of Berchidda in the Gallura region. Our family and their family, the Raus, have been friends since Mannoi Loi first went bartering around the island in his ox cart. Today, I consider the town my Sardinian home away from home, and on one of my visits, Giampiero made this dish for me at his house. What I loved about it is the way it uses the ingredients to create both the filling and the sauce (which makes a multipart recipe far less difficult). The result is so delicious and, dare I say it, sensual that sometimes four dozen ravioli are still not enough.

◈　◈　◈

On a clean workspace, mound the flour with a well in the center. Dissolve a pinch of salt in ¾ cup warm water. Add 1 egg and salted water into the well and gradually mix into the flour with your hands. When mixture begins to come together, add the lard and knead to fully incorporate. Let dough rest for an hour.

Heat olive oil in a large saucepan over medium heat. Add onion and garlic and cook until softened. Add lamb, thyme, bay leaves, and a pinch each of salt and freshly ground black pepper. Cook until lamb is browned, stirring frequently. Add white wine and deglaze pan. Stir in ¼ cup of the tomato puree and cook for 2 minutes for flavors to combine. Pour in beef stock, remaining tomato puree and peas; season with salt to taste. Simmer for 15 minutes. Remove from heat.

In a bowl, combine 2 cups of lamb sauce, the ricotta cheese, and 2 tablespoons of the pecorino. Set aside.

Roll the pasta through a pasta machine or with a roller. Cut into rounds, each 2 inches in diameter. In a small bowl, mix the remaining egg with a fork to make an egg wash.

Lightly brush the edges of the pasta rounds with the egg wash and then spoon the ricotta mixture into the center. Top with another pasta round and press edges well to seal; the pasta and filling should yield about 48 ravioli.

Cook ravioli in salted boiling water until they begin to float, 5 to 7 minutes. Return remaining sauce to medium heat and serve with ravioli, sprinkled with remaining pecorino cheese.

3 cups durum flour

Sea salt

2 eggs

4 ounces lard (or vegetable shortening)

2 tablespoons extra virgin olive oil

1 medium red onion, diced

2 garlic cloves, minced

2 pounds lamb shoulder, trimmed and diced

6 sprigs thyme, leaves only

2 bay leaves

Freshly ground black pepper

1 cup dry white wine

1 cup tomato puree

¾ cup beef stock

1 cup green peas, shelled

½ cup sheep's milk ricotta cheese (or other creamy ricotta cheese)

½ cup grated Pecorino Sardo cheese (or other pecorino cheese)

1 bunch flat leaf parsley, finely chopped

MY SECOND HOME (BERCHIDDA)

Aside from mentioning a well-regarded Vermentino vineyard and some nice mountain architecture, you won't find much on Berchidda in the guidebooks. A small town in the heart of the Gallura region of northern Sassari, it is perhaps best known as the home of the jazz trumpeter, Paolo Fresu, and his "Time in Jazz" festival. This relative obscurity suits me just fine. When I go to Berchidda, I escape to a place that seems as if it has been the same for centuries. Its flat land, framed by small hills and mountains, is home to generations of shepherds and winemakers.

Here, my friend Massimo still milks 250 sheep a day by hand, and my friend Pasquale's family distills ancient spirits like filu'e ferru and mirto. When I was last there, I joined the two of them at Massimo's family "home" in the hills. In the 1800s, each family in Berchidda (about 300 total) was given a small plot of mountain land on which to grow vegetables, make wine, keep animals, and store equipment and extra food. They built small shelters to shield them from the weather. During the hot summer months, families slept in their shelters, seeking out the cooler mountain air. But even in Berchidda times change. Many families do not need to keep animals or store equipment anymore. Today, families like Massimo's have turned the shelters into small homes—usually no more than one big, open room around a great fireplace with some storage in the back where they entertain friends and family. In other words, they have replaced the past with one of our most traditional ideals: hospitality.

Nettle ravioli with branzino and ricotta
Anzelottos de Orticata

SERVES 4

Zia Maria created a recipe that makes my archenemy in the fields—stinging nettles—a friend to my stomach. The nettles grow wild all around Orosei and no other wild green is this nasty. No matter how careful I was when wearing shorts by the Cedrino River or alongside our gardens, those troublemaking nettles found a way to get me. And they really do sting! The only salve was the oil found in the round leaves of marmaredda (malva in Italian). Today when I eat this dish at Zia Maria's restaurant, the nettles seem so peaceful, not to mention tasty, when combined with a little branzino in ravioli. Plus, they are loaded with protein. You can find them in many American farmers' markets, but if not, substitute the always nonviolent parsley.

◇　◇　◇

Blanch nettles in lightly salted boiling water. Transfer to bowl filled with ice water to stop the cooking process. Drain well and mince the cooked nettles; set aside.

Heat 2 tablespoons of olive oil over medium heat. Add garlic and shallot; cook until translucent. Add branzino and cook for 3 minutes. Pour in white wine and cook until liquids are absorbed. Stir in parsley, tomatoes, and salt and pepper to taste. Remove from heat and let cool. Transfer to a bowl and break up any large pieces with a fork. Add the ricotta and blend well to make a homogenous mixture.

On a clean workspace, mound the flour with a well in the center. Add 4 eggs, the nettles, and pinch of salt into the well and gradually mix into the flour with your hands. When mixture begins to come together, add the remaining 2 tablespoons of olive oil and knead to fully incorporate.

Roll the pasta to a $1/8$-inch thickness through a pasta machine or with a rolling pin. Cut into squares, each 2½ inches wide. In a small bowl, mix the remaining egg with a fork to make an egg wash. Lightly brush the edges of half of the pasta squares with the egg wash, and then spoon the ricotta mixture into the center. Top each with another pasta square and press edges well to seal; the pasta and filling should yield about 24 ravioli.

Cook ravioli in salted boiling water until they begin to float, 5 to 7 minutes.

Serve with sauce of your choice. (I suggest a simple sauce of cherry tomatoes, garlic, and dill simmered with white wine.)

1 bunch nettles (or flat leaf parsley)
4 tablespoons extra virgin olive oil
2 garlic cloves, minced
1 shallot, minced
1 pound branzino fillets, skinless, cleaned, and cut into ½-inch strips
½ cup dry white wine
1 tablespoon finely chopped parsley
2 Roma tomatoes, peeled, seeded, and chopped
Sea salt and freshly ground black pepper
½ cup sheep's milk ricotta cheese (or other creamy ricotta cheese)
3 cups durum flour
5 eggs

Half-moon ravioli with herbed ricotta cheese
Gulurjones de Recottu
SERVES 4

In my family, Zia Mary is the *pasta maker and my favorites are her raviolis, especially her sweet ravioli (see page 236) and these savory gulurjones. Gulurjones are semicircular ravioli filled with fresh cheese and are a specialty of the Ogliastra region, which lies to the south of Orosei. My aunt's version here uses ricotta, but her other ravioli fillings might include vegetables like Swiss chard. When she brought them over, we ravenously devoured every batch with only a plain tomato sauce and grated Pecorino Sardo on top.*

◇   ◇   ◇

In a bowl, combine ricotta, pecorino, 1 egg, parsley, marjoram, and nutmeg. Stir well and season with salt and pepper to taste. Set aside, refrigerating until ready to use.

On a clean workspace, mound the flour with a well in the center. Add 4 eggs and pinch of salt into the well and gradually mix into the flour with your hands. When mixture begins to come together, add the olive oil and knead to fully incorporate.

Roll the pasta to a $1/8$-inch thickness through a pasta machine or with a rolling pin. Cut into rounds, each 3 inches in diameter.

In a small bowl, mix the remaining egg with a fork to make an egg wash. Lightly brush the edges of the pasta rounds with the egg wash and then spoon the ricotta mixture into the center. Fold the rounds in half and press edges well to seal; should yield about 24 semicircular ravioli.

Cook ravioli in salted boiling water until they begin to float, 5 to 7 minutes.

2 cups sheep's milk ricotta cheese (or other creamy ricotta cheese)

4 ounces Pecorino Sardo cheese (or other pecorino cheese)

6 eggs

1 tablespoon finely chopped flat leaf parsley

1 tablespoon finely chopped marjoram

1 pinch nutmeg

Sea salt and freshly ground black pepper

3 cups durum flour

2 tablespoons extra virgin olive oil

ZIA MARY'S MACARRONES

Zia Mary's hair, apron, and kitchen table were always dusted with flour. Growing up, it seemed to me she was constantly kneading, rolling, filling, cutting, and trimming pasta. As a boy, I stood in her kitchen, ready to help, and thought she looked like a wonderful friendly ghost—her white apron standing out against the black curtains. With only a little sunlight and a small light bulb to guide us, her dining table became a work zone, and I got to knead the dough and get covered in flour, too. Simply put, pasta was the way Zia Mary showed her love, and making pasta with her was pure joy. "Great macarrones, Zia," we'd say after every bite, which is the only thanks she ever needed—besides a kiss.

Lorighittas with broccoli
Lorighittas Virdes

SERVES 4

When I visit my friends in Oristano, I always enjoy a plate of this signature Sardinian pasta shape. Lorighittas hail from the town of Morgongiori in the western part of the island and are not nearly as common as malloreddus or fregula. No wonder. They are far more intricate: a long, thin spaghetti noodle looped and braided to look like a small rope. The shape is ideally suited to pesto or seafood pasta with shellfish–anything that goes well with shell-shaped pasta. While lorighittas can stand up to whole broccoli florets, I prefer to mince the broccoli to better harmonize with the pasta and balance the other flavors in the dish, particularly the smokiness of the pancetta.

◈ ◈ ◈

Boil the broccoli in lightly salted boiling water for 5 minutes. Transfer immediately to a bowl of ice water to stop the cooking process. Drain well and mince broccoli. Set aside.

Boil the pasta in salted boiling water for 10 to 12 minutes, or until al dente.

While pasta is cooking, heat olive oil in a medium saucepan over medium heat. Add garlic, shallot, and pancetta, stirring until pancetta browns. Add broccoli and season to taste; toss well. Stir in ½ cup of pasta cooking liquid; reduce heat to medium-low and simmer for 10 minutes.

Add pasta to sauce and toss well. Remove from heat and mix in the pecorino cheese, stirring to incorporate.

1½ pounds broccoli florets
1 pound lorighittas pasta (or shell-shaped pasta)
4 tablespoons extra virgin olive oil
5 garlic cloves, minced
1 shallot, minced
¼ pound pancetta, minced
½ cup grated Pecorino Sardo cheese (or other pecorino cheese)

Sardinian paella
Paella e Fregula Sarda
SERVES 4

The first recipe that comes to mind when I think of fregula is traditional: fregula kin arsellas (see page 67). But then, I use fregula in many different dishes: in cold salads, as pasta to accompany capesante kin fregula e taffaranu (see page 82), or in this Sardinian paella recipe from my friends Pietro and Donatella. They live in the western part of Sardinia near Oristano, where more than four centuries of Spanish occupation left Catalan influences that are still very prominent today. Unlike traditional Spanish paella, it uses fregula instead of rice, only fresh seafood (no chorizo), and a robust fish stock that Pietro makes from the fish he gets from local fishermen at the Stagno di Cabras and the Golfo di Oristano.

◇　◇　◇

Heat fish stock in a large pot over medium heat. Rinse clams and mussels thoroughly to remove impurities.

In a paella pan or extra large saucepan, heat olive oil over medium heat. Add onion and cook until translucent. Add fregula and stir continuously for 2 minutes. Add clams and mussels. Stir saffron into 1 cup of the hot stock and add to pan, stirring continuously with a wooden spoon until clams and mussels begin to open, about 5 minutes. Add the wine and simmer for a few minutes longer.

Stir in fava beans, bell peppers, fresh and sun-dried tomatoes; then add bay leaves, thyme, and rosemary. Cook for 5 minutes, gradually ladling in stock as it is absorbed, continuing to stir constantly with a wooden spoon.

Add scampi, shrimp, calamari, monkfish, and dill; season to taste with salt. Toss well to combine. Continue to ladle in remaining stock gradually until all liquids are absorbed (about 5 minutes longer). Serve immediately.

4 cups fish stock (see recipe, page 68)

16 clams

16 mussels

4 tablespoons extra virgin olive oil

1 medium white onion, diced

2 cups fregula

½ teaspoon saffron

1 cup Vernaccia di Oristano wine (or dry sherry)

1 cup shelled fresh fava beans (or fresh or frozen green peas)

1 red bell pepper, julienned

1 green bell pepper, julienned

3 Roma tomatoes, seeded and diced

½ cup sun-dried tomatoes, chopped

2 bay leaves

5 sprigs thyme

1 sprig rosemary

4 ounces scampi (or baby langoustine), shell on, cut into 2 to 3 pieces

4 ounces medium shrimp, shell and heads on

4 ounces calamari, cleaned and chopped into 1-inch pieces

4 ounce fillet of monkfish (or flounder), cut into 2-inch pieces

½ bunch dill, coarsely chopped

Sea salt

FREGULA

Fregula—small, toasted semolina pasta—comes to Sardinia from the North African cuisine of the Maghreb. The Ligurians imported fregula from Tabarka (now part of Tunisia) through the Sardinian island of San Pietro, and it remains one of the few Moorish ingredients in our traditional cuisine. The name comes from the Latin word "*fricare*," which means to crumble, and that's what it looks like: crumbled bits of handmade pasta that bear some resemblance to Israeli couscous. In Orosei, we called fregula "*su ministru*" (little pieces), which we used in soups. I remember Mannai Vardeu making it start to finish by hand, her baskets of little grains drying outside on a sunny day. Today, fregula is still mostly handmade the way my friends Pietro and Donatella make it in their shop in the small town of Riola near Oristano. While they use a machine to knead the large quantities of dough and cut it into small pieces, they still complete the process by hand. First, they take the cut pasta and mix it with extra water and flour to give it a rustic coating. The pieces are then sifted through a *setaccio* (sieve), placed on a tray to dry, and toasted twice before they are ready to eat.

Fregula with asparagus and Gorgonzola
Fregula kin Isparau e Gorgonzola
SERVES 4

Making fregula in the style of risotto is not only tasty, but also takes half the work and time of traditional risotto. Though you still have to stir constantly, it takes only ten minutes to make, and while you still need to add hot stock, you add it all at once rather than a little at a time. The result is a fun variation on traditional risotto—perfect for a weeknight meal. Of course, Gorgonzola is not Sardinian in origin; it's from Piedmont in Italy. But I "discovered" it in Sardinia at the same time as fregula, and let's not forget that Piedmont and Sardinia were once part of the original Regno di Sardegna (Kingdom of Sardinia). So you'll forgive me this one concession to ingredients from the mainland.

◈   ◈   ◈

Heat the olive oil in a large saucepan over medium heat. Add the chopped shallot and sauté until golden. Add the asparagus and keep stirring for about 3 minutes longer.

In another pot, bring the chicken stock to a boil.

Add the fregula to the asparagus and cook for 2 minutes longer, letting the fregula toast, stirring continuously. Pour in the white wine and cook until liquids are absorbed.

Add the boiling chicken stock to the saucepan. Cook for 10 minutes or until liquid is fully absorbed, continuously stirring. Remove from heat. Stir in the Gorgonzola until fully incorporated, then stir in the single-orchard olive oil. Season with salt and pepper to taste. Let the mixture rest for a few minutes before serving.

2 tablespoons extra virgin olive oil

1 shallot, finely chopped

1 medium bunch asparagus, thinly sliced

4 cups chicken stock

2 cups fregula (see page 119)

½ cup Vermentino wine (or other dry white wine)

½ cup Gorgonzola, crumbled

2 tablespoons single-orchard extra virgin olive oil (see page 40)

Sea salt and freshly ground black pepper

Macarrones de busa with chicken livers and passito wine
Busa kin Icatos de Puddu

SERVES 4

Chicken is not served as often in Sardinia as meat (see recipes, pages 203–208). But when my mother and grandmother did kill a chicken for dinner, they of course reserved the liver and heart to turn into another meal. Sometimes they sautéed them with onions, but I loved when they made this pasta sauce using passitu (passito in Italian). Passitu is wine made from grapes that have dried before pressing (the name means to "dry out"). When aged it is called rosóliu, which only appears in the best vintage years and is served on special occasions like baptisms. Passitu has a concentrated sweetness that mixes with the chicken liver, onion, and sun-dried tomatoes to create a delightful, gravylike sauce. Its thickness is perfectly suited for another signature Sardinian pasta shape: macarrones de busa, a long, hollow noodle made by pressing the dough around a knitting needle. (Busa means "knitting needle" in Sardo.)

◊   ◊   ◊

Heat olive oil in a sauté pan over medium-high heat. Add onion, garlic cloves, celery, and bay leaf and cook until softened. Add chicken livers and cook until brown.

Deglaze the pan with the passito. Add veal stock, tomato paste, and sun-dried tomatoes. Stir in parsley and salt to taste.

Simmer over a low heat for 15 to 20 minutes, or until thickened. Remove bay leaf and garlic cloves; discard.

Cook pasta in salted boiling water for 10 to 15 minutes, or until al dente. Drain and add pasta to sauce. Serve sprinkled with the pecorino cheese.

¼ cup extra virgin olive oil
1 white onion, julienned
5 garlic cloves
1 stalk celery, diced
1 bay leaf
½ pound chicken livers, sliced
½ cup passito wine (or any dry sweet wine)
1 cup veal stock (or vegetable stock)
1½ tablespoons tomato paste
5 sun-dried tomatoes, thinly sliced
½ bunch flat leaf parsley, chopped
Sea salt
12 ounces macarrones de busa pasta (or bucatini pasta)
2 tablespoons grated Pecorino Sardo cheese (or other pecorino cheese)

ZIA MARIA'S MACARRONES DE BUSA

Whenever I have a chance to cook with Zia Maria (above, left), we always make her macarrones de busa. It is our little tradition that started more than twenty years ago, when I helped in her restaurant. The beauty of her macarrones de busa is in the precise way she makes them, and I always make sure I follow her lead. First, she kneads dough made from flour, water, salt, and maybe some saffron until it is "warm." She rolls out long strands of dough and then pulls pieces exactly as long as from the tip of her thumb to her knuckle. Finally, she rolls the pieces around a bicycle spoke to create noodles with fine hollow centers that allow some sauce to get inside and lays them in a basket to dry. (Zia Maria prefers the finer centers created by the spoke to the knitting needle, but the overall effect is the same.) Until recently, Zia Maria made her own macarrones de busa everyday for Su Barchile's signature pasta dish with lobster. These days, she is too busy running the bustling restaurant and inn to make enough macarrones de busa to satisfy her guests. Several women from Orosei make it for her. But like me, they had better make sure to follow her lead.

Pasta with meat ragù
Macarrones kin Bagna e Petha
SERVES 4

Ragù is an Italian term for a thick meat sauce often finished with grated cheese. In my home, my mother made ragù from the cuts of beef, pork, or lamb remaining from the week, along with the last drops from a bottle of wine and whatever vegetables we had lying around. No matter the combination of ingredients, she cooked them together to make this wonderful, complex sauce—a great example of how nothing goes to waste in Sardinia. To make this sauce today, ask your butcher for shoulder meat, which is inexpensive and most similar to the pieces we had left in our house. A ragù cooks slowly in order to tenderize the chunks of meat and get all the flavor of the meat into the sauce. This ragù is best served with tubular pasta like macarrones de busa so the sauce can coat the pasta inside and out.

◊   ◊   ◊

Heat olive oil, garlic, and bay leaves in a large saucepan over medium heat. Add meat and brown evenly. Add the wine and stir to incorporate, 2 to 3 minutes.

Add celery, carrot, shallots, sun-dried tomatoes, and pepperoncini to the saucepan. In a bowl, crush canned tomatoes with a food mill or a fork, discarding any unripened pieces, and add with juices to saucepan. Tie myrtle leaves, sage, and thyme into a bouquet and secure with kitchen twine; add to the saucepan. Season to taste with salt and pepper, stir well, and cook covered for 15 minutes. Reduce heat to low and simmer, covered, 15 minutes longer, stirring occasionally to prevent sticking.

Cook pasta in salted boiling water for 10 to 15 minutes, or until al dente. Drain and add cooked pasta to sauce, tossing well to combine. Discard herb bouquet and bay leaves. Stir in cheese before serving.

4 tablespoons extra virgin olive oil

1 garlic clove, minced

2 bay leaves

4 ounces beef shoulder, trimmed and chopped

4 ounces lamb shoulder, trimmed and chopped

4 ounces pork shoulder, trimmed and chopped

½ cup Vermentino wine (or other dry white wine)

1 stalk celery, chopped

1 carrot, chopped

2 shallots, chopped

½ cup sun-dried tomatoes, julienned

2 fresh pepperoncini, halved (or 2 pinches of crushed red pepper)

1 can (14.5 ounce) peeled plum tomatoes, undrained

2 sprigs myrtle leaves (see page 231)

2 sprigs sage

2 sprigs thyme

Sea salt and freshly ground black pepper

1 pound macarrones de busa (or other tubular pasta, like bucatini)

1 cup grated Pecorino Sardo cheese (or other pecorino cheese)

Pasta with ricotta, saffron, and bitter honey
Macarrones kin Taffaranu e Mele

SERVES 4

The shepherd who used our land for grazing gave my family what Sardinians call a "ransom." In the spring, he gave us a lamb; for Easter, he brought some fresh cheese for the seadas (see page 226); and throughout the year, he offered us some of his best ricotta for simple pasta dishes like macarrones kin recottu. I wanted to create a new recipe that not only honored this traditional dish but also used two other ancient ingredients—saffron and bitter honey—that we often use in other recipes with fresh ricotta. Mixed with sheep's milk, the ricotta becomes a thick sauce that is both familiar and different, enhancing the flavors of all the ingredients. The sauce calls for malloreddus, but you can use any small pasta shape that can be coated with the sauce, drizzled with warm bitter honey, and then eaten with a spoon.

◇ ◇ ◇

Bring a large pot of salted water to a boil, add pasta and boil for 10 to 15 minutes, or until al dente.

While pasta is cooking, melt the butter in a large pan over medium heat, stirring continuously. Add milk and ricotta, stirring until well incorporated. Add saffron, stirring to infuse the sauce, about 3 minutes. Remove from heat.

In a small saucepan over low heat, warm the bitter honey. Stir occasionally to prevent burning.

Drain pasta and add to ricotta mixture, toss well over medium heat. Add salt and pepper to taste. Pour into a ceramic serving bowl, then stir in warmed bitter honey and toss to combine. Serve immediately.

1 pound malloreddus pasta (see page 95)
½ cup (1 stick) unsalted butter
1 cup milk (preferably sheep or goat's milk)
1 cup sheep's milk ricotta cheese (or other creamy ricotta cheese)
½ to 1 teaspoon saffron
½ cup bitter honey (see page 229)
Sea salt and freshly ground black pepper

SAFFRON

Sardinia is known for the high quality of its saffron, but its origins on the island are unclear. Some believe it dates back to the Phoenicians; others think the Romans cultivated it. All I know is that, growing up, we got our saffron from Monreale near Oristano and it was always in our pantry. We added its delicate flavor to our pastas, soups, and even desserts. But we used it sparingly, not only because a little goes a long way but also because saffron is expensive— and deservingly so. Each strand of saffron is the stigma from a purple crocus. The price we pay is for the exhausting and seemingly endless work of harvesting the strands one at a time by hand; it takes around 4,000 stigmas to make an ounce of saffron.

Spaghetti with garlic and skinless tomatoes
Ispaghittos kin Azu

SERVES 4

This is an especially easy dish, one that must be made when tomatoes are in season. This version has a little more garlic and olive oil than the version my mother made, but it still captures our way of eating spaghetti and tomatoes without a thick pile of sauce to hide the flavor of the herbs and olive oil. I call them skinless tomatoes because my mother made this dish at the end of the season when the tomatoes were heavy and ripe and the skin came right off. If you have a farmers' market that sells tomatoes in the fall, you know the fruit I mean.

◇   ◇   ◇

Cook pasta in salted boiling water for 10 to 15 minutes, or until al dente.

While pasta is cooking, heat olive oil in a large saucepan over medium heat. Add garlic and cook until garlic is softened. Stir in the pepperoncino. Add the tomato strips, tossing well to combine flavors. Let cook for 15 minutes, adding some of the pasta cooking liquid if necessary.

Add parsley to tomato sauce, stirring to incorporate. Drain pasta and add to sauce, tossing well. Finish with a sprinkling of pecorino cheese and chopped basil.

1 pound spaghetti

⅓ cup extra virgin olive oil

8 garlic cloves, coarsely chopped

1 fresh pepperoncino, chopped (or 1 pinch of crushed red pepper)

2 pounds Roma tomatoes, peeled, seeded, and cut into strips

1 bunch flat leaf parsley, roughly chopped

¼ cup grated Pecorino Sardo cheese (or other pecorino cheese)

2 sprigs basil, chopped

Spaghetti with bottarga
Ispaghittos kin Buttariga

SERVES 4

*S*ardinia remains a barter society today, as we think nothing of trading fruit, vegetables, meat, cheese, or wine with our neighbors. ("Oh, you have fava beans? I'll give you some nice fennel.") But for my grandparents, bartering was a way of life. My mother used to tell me that when she saw Mannai Vardeu packing water, pane carasau, and other food into sa bertula (a sheep's wool saddlebag with black and white stripes that Mannoi Loi carried over his shoulder or on the side of the cart), she knew it was time for my grandfather to leave on his journey. He would take the ox cart and fill it with products from our orchards and head out for a two-week "business trip" to different parts of the island. He went south to Nuoro and Cagliari, west into the mountains toward Oristano, and through Campidano Plain in the middle of the island. Along the way, he bartered with shepherds and farmers for produce and pecorino, but his real prizes were soap and bottarga. When my grandfather got back home, he immediately asked for this dish.

◈   ◈   ◈

Bring a large pot of salted water to a boil, add pasta and boil for 10 to 15 minutes, or until al dente.

While pasta is cooking, heat olive oil in a saucepan over medium heat. Add garlic and cook until browned to flavor the oil. Remove garlic and discard. Lower heat to medium-low and stir in 1 tablespoon of butter and 1 tablespoon of bottarga. Add pasta and toss well to coat.

Remove from heat and stir in remaining butter, another tablespoon of bottarga, and the parsley. Toss to coat evenly.

Serve sprinkled with the remaining bottarga.

1 pound spaghetti
4 tablespoons extra virgin olive oil
6 garlic cloves, cracked
2 tablespoons unsalted butter
4 tablespoons grated bottarga di muggine
    (see page 30)
1 tablespoon finely chopped flat leaf parsley

"A CHENT'ANNOS" ("MAY YOU LIVE TO ONE HUNDRED")

Mannoi Loi lived a robust life until he died at the age of 107. In other words, a baby. Okay, maybe he was no longer crossing the island in an ox cart, but he was far from alone in Sardinia in his centenarian status. *National Geographic* reported in November 2005 that "residents of Okinawa, Sardinia, and Loma Linda, California, live longer, healthier lives than just about anyone else on Earth." Specifically, researchers found an amazing percentage of men and women on the island living to 100. What is the Sardinian secret? The magazine mentioned several reasons for the longevity—healthy diets filled with fresh foods and good fats, a simpler lifestyle and deep family bonds, as well as strong ties to the land, which remains remarkably undeveloped.

Spaghetti with pecorino and bottarga
Ispaghittos a sa Tabarkina

Like my father, when I travel and hear about a recipe or taste something new, I immediately write it down to preserve the memory. But I didn't need my notes to remember this dish. It is based on a traditional recipe from the town of Carloforte on the island of San Pietro, home to some of Sardinia's finest tuna fishermen (see page 195). What struck me was the way the dish used two contrasting staples of Sardinian cuisine—the pecorino of the shepherds and the bottarga of the fisherman. The original dish calls for tuna bottarga, which is more common in the Mediterranean, especially in North Africa. It has a stronger flavor than the delicate Sardinian grey mullet bottarga I prefer.

Bring a large pot of salted water to a boil, add pasta, and boil for 10 to 15 minutes, or until al dente.

While pasta is cooking, heat the 2 tablespoons of olive oil in a medium saucepan over medium heat. Add onion and garlic and cook until softened. Add tomatoes, bay leaf, and parsley. Bring mixture to a boil. Add the wine and stir to incorporate. Let cook for 5 minutes, stirring often to prevent sticking.

Remove from heat and stir bottarga into the tomato sauce. Discard bay leaf. Drain pasta, add to the sauce, and toss to combine. Stir in chives and the fruttato extra virgin olive oil. Finish with pecorino cheese.

1 pound thin spaghetti

2 tablespoons extra virgin olive oil

1 extra large green onion, diced

2 garlic cloves, minced

1 can (14.5 ounce) tomato strips

1 bay leaf

1 bunch flat leaf parsley, finely chopped

⅓ cup Vermentino wine (or other dry white wine)

⅓ cup grated bottarga di muggine (see page 30)

1 tablespoon finely chopped chives

3 tablespoons fruttato extra virgin olive oil (see page 40)

½ cup grated Pecorino Sardo cheese (or other pecorino cheese)

UNA TASSA E VINU (A GLASS OF WINE)

Sardinians take wine seriously: It is an essential ingredient to who we are. Wine in Sardinia is as old as pane carasau and bottarga and dates back to the Romans and Phoenicians. While there are an ever-growing number of large-scale vineyards and bottlers, many families still make their own wine to serve family and friends at celebrations or to welcome guests, and single family vineyards passed down for generations (like my father's) still dot the island's roads like a patchwork quilt. Each family has its own style, tricks, and traditions (many use the Alberello form of cultivation, or small tree production), but all Sardinian vineyards (small and large) reflect the unique qualities of our ancient soil.

When I came to the United States and opened my first restaurant in Dallas in 1988, Sardinian wine was almost impossible to find. For myself, I carried all I could in my suitcases. For my customers, I imported what I could, but they could not buy it anywhere else and I could not send it home with them when they asked for more. Today, Sardinian wines are becoming more and more popular. The indigenous varieties—including Bovale Sardo, Cannonau, Carignano, Girò, Malvasia, Moscato, Monica, Nuragus, Oliena, Vermentino, and Vernaccia—have won international acclaim, and I am able to feature a large selection from across the island and even import wine from my family's orchards.

Sardinia's most popular red grape is Cannonau, which dates back to the Spanish occupation. The grapes are an indigenous form of Grenache and are grown all over the island, the best coming mostly from the heart of the island around Nuoro and Barbagia. Dry, robust, and earthy, this is a great wine to go with pastas (like Macarrones de Ariola, Anzelottos de Petha, or any hearty ragù), roasted and grilled meats (especially suckling pig), or a plate of assorted cheeses.

Vermentino is our most popular white grape. It is used to make Vermentino di Sardegna, a classic light, crisp white wine. Vermentino grapes are grown all over the island but especially along the coast, making it

an excellent pairing with our seafood. Vermentino di Gallura, one of my favorite whites in the world for its complexity and pleasing acidity, refers to a specific area of Vermentino production: Gallura in the northern part of the island. I prefer the Vermentino di Gallura from the Berchidda countryside in particular, for its dry and slightly bittersweet flavor. It makes an excellent pairing with the Issalata de Iscolliu (cold seafood salad), Paella e Fregula Sarda (Sardinian paella), or Piske a Sale (whole fish in rock salt). It's also great drunk just by itself on a sunny afternoon.

The other Sardinian wine that appears frequently in this book is harder to find beyond Sardinia: Vernaccia di Oristano. Grown in the Tirso basin's sandy gravelly soil (in the center-west of the island), Vernaccia grapes produce a sherry-like dry white wine with high alcohol content. In fact, after fermentation, the wine is traditionally aged in chestnut barrels for more years than your average white wine. The process is similar to that of sherry production. The wine is transferred into smaller barrels each year, and the barrels are never filled to capacity, in order to allow a slower oxidation. What is considered a young Vernaccia would be a wine aged for at least two and a half years. A more aged Vernaccia would be a wine that has aged for as many as six years (the aging magnifies the flavor of the wine). This more aged type earns the title "riserva," and the vintage year is printed on the label. Young Vernaccia is great with bottarga dishes. Riserva can be enjoyed as an aperitif, paired with creamy pastas (like Rosu Cremosu), or even with desserts on the days of Sa Sartiglia (see page 237).

Sardinian wines are gaining ground in official classification these days. The Vermentino di Gallura varietal has earned the highest distinction in the world of Italian wine—DOCG (Denominazióne di Origine Controllata e Garantita). This designation serves as a guarantee of a wine's quality. A DOCG wine must come from grapes grown in a defined area, it must be produced with traditional methods, and it must be tested regularly. Only twenty varietals in Italy have attained this status. The next highest class of Italian wines are called DOC wines, and the three other varietals discussed above fall into this category—Vermentino di Sardegna, Cannonau, and Vernaccia di Oristano. DOC wines are produced under the same rules as DOCG wines but do not require the approval of a tasting panel before bottling. Sardinia also has another 16 wines in the next classification below DOC, which is IGT (*Indicazione Geografica Tipica*, wines produced in a specific area). No other region in Italy has as many wines that meet this category. If all this is not enough to get you drinking, consider this: A study in the British journal *Nature* found that our red grapes had the highest levels of procyanidin, which is responsible for the well-documented heart benefits of red wine.

Spaghetti with sea urchin
Ispaghittos kin Ovos de Erithu
SERVES 4

I find sea urchin's creamy texture and saltwater flavor both elegant and sexy–a delicacy in every way. I like to eat it raw, just like the fishermen of Olbia (see page 61). But even people who do not eat sea urchin raw love it in this dish, a specialty in Olbia. Spaghetti is a perfect pairing with sea urchin–its long strands an ideal vehicle for the roe's creaminess. This preparation is similar to pasta carbonara in that the sea urchin is "cooked" when tossed with the hot spaghetti the way the egg is in a carbonara. Each piece ends up lightly coated with roe so you taste its sultriness in every bite. One suggestion: Opening sea urchins is a messy job even for the experienced shucker. There will be urchin spine fragments everywhere. If you are buying your sea urchins in the shell, I suggest you open them over the sink.

◈   ◈   ◈

Bring a large pot of salted water to a boil, add pasta and boil for 10 to 15 minutes, or until al dente.

In a bowl, whisk together sea urchin roe, 2 tablespoons of the olive oil, chives, and salt and pepper to taste.

Heat remaining 2 tablespoons of olive oil in a medium saucepan over medium heat. Add garlic and cook until golden. Remove garlic and discard. Add cooked pasta to the saucepan and toss well to coat.

Remove from heat and add sea urchin sauce, tossing well. Serve immediately.

1 pound spaghetti
½ pound sea urchin roe
4 tablespoons extra virgin olive oil
½ bunch chives, finely chopped
Sea salt and freshly ground black pepper
4 garlic cloves, cracked

Spaghetti with crabmeat and tomato sauce
Ispaghittos kin Cavaros

SERVES 4

This recipe comes from Zia Maria and Zio Pietro. My uncle loved the sea and was an expert at harpooning fish. He would spend all his free time at the shore and developed great relationships with local fishermen, who drank at their pagoda on the beach (see page 184). So when they opened their restaurant, Su Barchile, more than 30 years ago, these fishermen provided him with the freshest local fish and shellfish. I helped at the restaurant during the summertime, just as I had at the pagoda and fell in love with this recipe, one of their signature dishes today. It is my favorite recipe for preparing the tiny granchi di fiume crab, which comes from around Orosei, or the equally delicious (and meaty, but hairy-looking) Pelosa crab, which thrives around the rocks of Oristano.

◇ ◇ ◇

Blanch crabs in salted boiling water. Transfer immediately to bowl filled with ice water to cool and stop the cooking process. (If using blue crab, cut off ends of legs and cut bodies into 4 to 6 pieces each. Rinse under running water.)

Heat 2 tablespoons of olive oil and garlic in a large saucepan over medium-high heat. Add crabs and sauté for a minute. Pour in filu'e ferru and light on fire to cook off the alcohol.

Reserve 2 tablespoons of the parsley. Add the remaining parsley, oregano, pepperoncino, and teardrop tomatoes and stir for flavors to combine. Pour in tomato sauce and fish stock; season with salt to taste. Simmer for 15 minutes.

Cook spaghetti in salted boiling water for 10 to 15 minutes, or until al dente. Drain pasta and add to sauce and toss well. Sprinkle with reserved parsley and finish with a drizzling of remaining 2 tablespoons olive oil.

1 pound granchi di fiume crab (or 5 or 6 female blue crabs), cleaned

4 tablespoons extra virgin olive oil

6 garlic cloves, minced

¼ cup filu'e ferru (see page 170) (or grappa or brandy)

1 bunch of parsley, chopped

2 sprigs oregano

2 fresh pepperoncino (or ½ teaspoon crushed red pepper)

1 cup teardrop tomatoes (or cherry tomatoes), halved

1 cup tomato sauce (see recipe, page 92)

½ cup fish stock (see recipe, page 68)

Sea salt

1 pound spaghetti

The pasta of the cattleman
Macarrones de Massaju

SERVES 4

"Massaja vona si viet I' su pacu!" say the men of Sardinia: literally, "A capable woman is revealed when using very little." Growing up, we often did not have a lot, and with the men away for days at a time working, bartering, or tending the fields, women ran every part of the home. They took care of the finances, watched over the children, cooked the meals, and everything in between. In other words, they did a lot with a little. Mannai Carta could make dinner with one egg and a little fresh cheese and make my grandfather happy. The cattleman's wife would do the same with his ingredients in this recipe, including making the fresh cheese from a bucket of milk he brought her.

◇　◇　◇

Cook the pasta in salted boiling water for 10 to 15 minutes, or until al dente.

Heat olive oil in a saucepan over medium heat. Add garlic and cook until golden. Add the tomatoes and parsley. Add the pasta and salt to taste and toss well.

Place the pasta in a serving bowl and toss with the fresh mozzarella and basil.

1 pound penne pasta
¼ cup extra virgin olive oil
4 garlic cloves, thinly sliced
6 Roma tomatoes, peeled, drained, seeded, and cut into ½-inch strips
1 tablespoon chopped flat leaf parsley
Sea salt
4 ounces fresh mozzarella cheese, cubed
3 sprigs basil, chopped

CASIZZOLU

Casizzolu is fresh cow's milk cheese traditionally made from milk of the "red cow" of Montiferru near Oristano (see page 172). In Sardinia, casizzolu and similar fresh cheeses made from cow's milk, such as taedda, are known as woman's cheese, because they are the only cheeses on the island made at home (which is to say, made by women). While the sheep were in the fields and the goats in the mountains, cows were kept in the courtyard. Every family had a cow for milk and cheese, but above all for work. Carts were our trucks, and cows were the engines to pull those carts and the men back and forth to the fields and beyond. (In the evening, a procession of cows and carts filled the bridge over the river as they headed back to town.) The men milked the cows in the morning before they left, and the women would take the bucket and process the curd to make the fresh cheese. They watched and waited for the precise moment to gather it, shape it into the traditional circular shape, tie it at

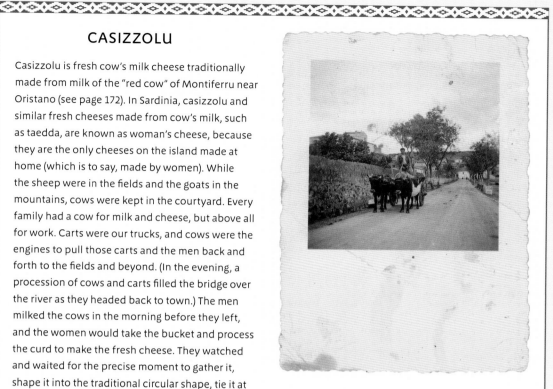

the top, and finally hang it in the home until it was ready. And though many factories make casizzolu today, you can still find it hanging in homes across Sardinia.

Cold pasta salad with baby artichokes
Pinninos kin Iscarzofa
SERVES 4

This is a dish I made during the start of summer while I was going to high school in Nuoro. I have a special fondness for it, because I first made it when I was single. I left a plate at the door for the girls who lived nearby and quickly learned the power of food. (A lesson I never forgot, as I met my wife while working in a restaurant!) This recipe is also a great showcase for baby artichokes. You could use either preserved or fresh artichokes in this recipe, but what makes the dish is the touch of ricotta salata at the end.

⬦　⬦　⬦

Clean and trim artichokes; cut in half lengthwise. Remove the choke, leaving the heart and tender bottom leaves. Place the halves into a bowl of cold water and lemon juice to prevent artichokes from turning black.

Drain artichokes and place in lightly salted boiling water for 10 minutes. Transfer to bowl filled with ice water immediately to stop the cooking process. Thinly slice artichoke hearts into ¼-inch slices and put into a bowl. Add tomatoes, basil, parsley, and garlic; toss well.

Bring a large pot of salted water to a boil, add pasta and boil for 10 to 15 minutes, or until al dente. Drain and rinse under cold running water to stop the cooking process. Transfer pasta to a serving bowl and toss with ¼ cup of the fruttato olive oil to prevent sticking.

Add the artichoke and tomato mixture to the pasta and pour in the remaining fruttato olive oil. Toss well and season to taste. Toss with the ricotta salata before serving.

1 pound baby artichokes
Juice of 1 lemon
2 cups yellow and red teardrop tomatoes (or cherry tomatoes), halved
1 bunch basil, chopped
½ bunch flat leaf parsley, chopped
6 garlic cloves, thinly sliced
1 pound penne pasta
¾ cup fruttato extra virgin olive oil (see page 40)
Sea salt and freshly ground black pepper
4 ounces ricotta salata cheese, shredded

BABY ARTICHOKES

Baby artichokes are not the first growth from the plant (what we call the *primizie*) but the last—the leftovers from the plant's final days. The first artichokes of the season come up in the middle of the stalk and look like kings of the plant. Through the spring and into summer, the artichokes grow on the side until the plant grows weak in the heat and starts to die. The little ones left behind are the baby artichokes—we eat them fresh (they require little trimming) but more often preserved in olive oil. They are perfect for this cold pasta salad.

Penne with red rock cod
Pinninos kin Bagna e Roccale
SERVES 4

When I was ten and old enough to go harpoon fishing with Zio Pietro, he took me to the rocks of the bay in Orosei, where we caught red rock cod. Quite possibly the ugliest fish you can eat (the fishermen who save it for me today call it "scorfano," or "not pretty"), it nevertheless tastes beautiful. Its delicate flavor is closest to grouper and red snapper but is distinguished by the essence of shellfish, which make up the bulk of its diet. We fillet it ourselves: preserving the liver for a delicious treat, reserving the head and bones to make stock, and using the meat for this recipe. Like many Sardinian recipes, little about making this dish is difficult and the method of preparation will be familiar: you cook the fish, add the ingredients and pasta, and toss it all together to make a nice summer dish with bright fish and herb flavor.

◈ ◈ ◈

Bring a large pot of salted water to a boil, add pasta and boil for 10 to 15 minutes, or until al dente.

While pasta is cooking, heat olive oil and minced garlic in a large saucepan over medium-low heat. Add fish and salt to taste, cooking for 2 minutes. Add the wine and cook until liquid is absorbed. Gently stir in tomatoes and basil, and then pour in fish stock. Bring to a boil, then add the oregano. Reduce heat to low and let simmer for 5 minutes.

Add pasta to the sauce and toss well to combine.

1 pound penne pasta
4 tablespoons extra virgin olive oil
2 garlic cloves, minced
1 pound red rock cod fillets (preferably skin on) (or grouper), cut into ½-inch strips
Sea salt
½ cup Vermentino wine (or other dry white wine)
2 cups cherry tomatoes, quartered
2 sprigs basil, chopped
½ cup fish stock (see recipe, page 68)
3 sprigs oregano

Fettuccini with seafood ragù
Alisanzas kin Piske

SERVES 4

As our seafaring tradition has developed, so has our taste for using seafood in the style of a ragù. Today, seafood ragùs can be found all over the island. And just like the cold seafood salad (see page 41), everyone has a different way of making it. Some use exact proportions of specific fish and shellfish. Some use whatever bounty the sea has to offer. Unlike my seafood salad, for which I prefer exact ingredients, I am more flexible with a ragù. I prefer to have clams and calamari, but will use whatever white fish is available. One thing is certain, though: seafood ragù is a "big" sauce and needs big macarrones like the long flat ribbons of fettuccini. Fettuccini is one of the oldest pastas on the island and is as suited for a simple sauce of tomato and basil as it is for this recipe, in which it balances the bites of seafood and absorbs the sauce. This dish is even better the second day, when the flavors have blended even more.

◇　◇　◇

In a bowl, crush canned tomatoes with a food mill or a fork, discarding any unripened pieces. Heat 2 tablespoons of olive oil in a saucepan over medium heat. Add onion and half of the garlic, mix well, and add pepperoncino and tomatoes with juices. Bring mixture to a boil; reduce heat to low. Simmer for 15 minutes.

Wash clams thoroughly with fresh water. Place clams in a large pot with ½ cup of water. Heat until clams open. Separate clams from juices, passing the juice through a sieve lined with cheesecloth to remove any sediment or impurities. Reserve juice; set clams aside and keep them warm.

Bring a large pot of salted water to a boil, add pasta and boil for 10 to 15 minutes, or until al dente.

While pasta is cooking, heat remaining 2 tablespoons of olive oil and remaining garlic in a large saucepan over medium heat. Add calamari, grouper, red snapper, thyme, and salt to taste. Cook for 5 minutes, stirring to cook fish evenly. Add the wine and cook until reduced by half. Stir in clams and filtered juices. Add tomato sauce, half of the parsley, and half of the chives. Reduce heat to low and let simmer for 10 minutes.

Add the cooked pasta to the sauce and toss well to combine. Stir in remaining herbs before serving.

1 can (14.5 ounce) peeled plum tomatoes, undrained

4 tablespoons extra virgin olive oil

1 extra large green onion, minced

2 cloves garlic, minced

1 fresh pepperoncino, chopped (or ½ to 1 teaspoon of crushed red pepper)

16 manilla clams

1 pound fettuccini pasta

4 ounces cleaned calamari, chopped

4 ounces grouper fillet (preferably skin on), chopped

4 ounces red snapper fillet (preferably skin on), chopped

4 sprigs thyme, leaves only

Sea salt

½ cup Vermentino wine (or other dry white wine)

½ bunch flat leaf parsley, finely chopped

½ bunch chives, finely chopped

Fettuccini with zucchini, zucchini blossoms, and bottarga
Alisanzas kin Curcurica e Buttariga

SERVES 4

In school, when someone failed a test or was held back, we said that person got "curcurica" (zucchini); instead of having a beautiful summer you had to work. "Zucchini." My father always grew zucchini in our garden and we happily ate them and the blossoms all season long. Poor zucchini—so easy to grow and yet the proverbial consolation prize for failure. My sister Angela and I thought about this contradiction one summer when I returned from the United States. We were inspired to create this dish using both the zucchini and its blossoms (which you can find in many farmers' markets and supermarkets) and bottarga with fish stock. The texture of the zucchini and fettuccini balance each other so nicely you'll be delighted to get "curcurica."

◈ ◈ ◈

Bring a large pot of salted water to a boil, add pasta and boil for 10 to 15 minutes, or until al dente.

While pasta is cooking, heat olive oil in a large saucepan over medium heat. Add garlic and cook until translucent. Add zucchini and sauté for 2 minutes. Pour in the wine and let it cook until reduced by half.

Stir in tomatoes and parsley and cook for 5 minutes longer. Add fish stock. Bring mixture to a boil, and then reduce heat to low. Add zucchini blossoms, 2 tablespoons of bottarga and butter, stir well to combine, and let simmer for 3 minutes. Season to taste.

Add cooked fettuccini to the sauce, tossing well. Pour pasta into serving dish and sprinkle with remaining 3 tablespoons of bottarga.

1 pound fettuccini pasta
4 tablespoons extra virgin olive oil
3 garlic cloves, thinly sliced
½ pound baby zucchini, thinly julienned
1 cup Vernaccia wine (or other dry white wine)
1 cup teardrop tomatoes (or cherry tomatoes), halved
½ bunch flat leaf parsley, finely chopped
1 cup fish stock (see recipe, page 68)
12 zucchini blossoms, chopped
5 tablespoons grated bottarga di muggine (see page 30)
4 tablespoons (½ stick) unsalted butter
Sea salt and freshly ground black pepper

Risotto with sausage and pecorino
Rosu kin Sartizza

SERVES 4

The sausage we made after killing a pig hung on hooks by the fireplace until it was dry and ready for slicing. Sometimes my mother pulled down a small piece before it was dried for pulenta kin sartizza (page 162). But we usually waited for a month or so for this classic Sardinian winter dish of Roma rice, sausage, and tomato sauce. Just the smell warms my bones and gives me strength to face the winter cold.

◇　　◇　　◇

In a medium saucepan over high heat, bring the beef stock to a boil. Reduce heat to low, keeping stock hot.

Heat 2 tablespoons of the extra virgin olive oil in a large saucepan over medium heat. Add half of the shallots and cook until translucent. Add sausage and sun-dried tomatoes and cook for 2 to 3 minutes. Pour in tomato puree and thyme; let simmer for 15 minutes.

In a thick-bottomed saucepan (copper is best), heat remaining 2 tablespoons of extra virgin olive oil over medium-high heat. Add remaining shallots and cook until translucent. Add the rice and stir continuously with a wooden spoon for 2 to 3 minutes. Add the wine, stirring until alcohol is evaporated.

Gradually ladle in the beef stock, stirring continuously with the wooden spoon, making sure the rice does not stick to the bottom of the pan. Add more stock as it is absorbed, stirring until rice is al dente and creamy, about 15 minutes. Add sausage sauce and stir until well combined. Add cold-pressed olive oil, stirring until creamy. Remove from heat and stir in the cheeses and the parsley.

4 cups beef stock

4 tablespoons extra virgin olive oil

2 shallots, diced

12 ounces dry aged sausage (or salami), diced

½ cup sun-dried tomatoes, chopped

1 can (14.5 ounce) pureed plum tomatoes, undrained

6 sprigs thyme, leaves only

2 cups Sardinian Roma rice (see page 153)

½ cup dry red wine

⅓ cup cold-pressed extra virgin olive oil

½ cup grated Pecorino Sardo stagionato cheese (or other aged pecorino cheese),

½ cup grated Pecorino Sardo semi-stagionato cheese (or other semi-aged pecorino cheese)

2 tablespoons finely chopped flat leaf parsley

ROSU

When I was feeling sick, especially in winter, Mannai Carta would say to my mother, "Give him a fistful of rice (*rosu*) to get him back on his feet." My mother would then give me a cup of steamed rice or just the broth she cooked the rice in—with all the starch from the grains, it filled me up when I was too weak to chew. It always worked. Today, even when I am feeling fine, I find comfort when I make risotto.

And yes, the rice we ate was Sardinian in origin and has been eaten on the island for centuries. It comes from the region surrounding Oristano where the low flood plains of the Tirso River valley, sea breezes, and mild temperatures are ideally suited for its growth. Large-scale production started when our friends Cesello and Alessio's family established the first rice factory in Oristano more than half a century ago. In true Sardinian fashion, they produce it just about the same way today.

When the rice comes in from the fields, a machine separates the grains from their skin and then sends them through another half-dozen machines to weed out the bad grains and clean and polish the good ones. The rice gets whiter and whiter and thinner and thinner along the way as it rubs against the sandpaperlike

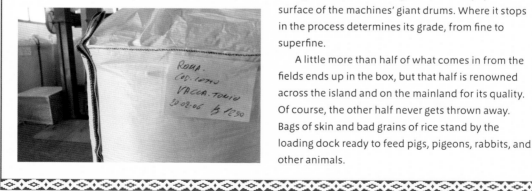

surface of the machines' giant drums. Where it stops in the process determines its grade, from fine to superfine.

A little more than half of what comes in from the fields ends up in the box, but that half is renowned across the island and on the mainland for its quality. Of course, the other half never gets thrown away. Bags of skin and bad grains of rice stand by the loading dock ready to feed pigs, pigeons, rabbits, and other animals.

Risotto with wild asparagus and pecorino
Rosu kin Isparau Agreste

SERVES 4

I *get carried away hunting wild asparagus. The hills of Orosei seduce me with a carpet of purple, yellow, and white wildflowers, not to mention wild dandelion and fennel. As I climb, the sound of sheep bells fills the air while the farmland, Cedrino River, and sea spread out behind me. It is always enough to make me forget I am poking my hands through the thorns of bramble and hawthorn to get the asparagus. Taking my happily scratched-up hands home, I find the first hot bite of this creamy risotto dish—a version of which you can find on many menus in the spring—the perfect way to wind down: a peaceful meal to end my day of hunting.*

In a medium saucepan over high heat, bring the chicken stock to a boil. Reduce heat to low, keeping stock hot.

In a medium saucepan, heat 2 tablespoons of olive oil over medium heat. Add half of the shallots and cook until softened. Add asparagus and season to taste. Stir in parsley. Add 1 cup of chicken stock and cook 2 to 3 minutes. Remove from heat and set aside.

In a thick-bottomed saucepan (copper is best), heat the remaining 2 tablespoons of olive oil over medium-high heat. Add remaining shallots and cook until translucent. Add the rice, stirring continuously with a wooden spoon for 2 to 3 minutes. Add the wine, stirring until evaporated. Reduce heat to medium.

Gradually ladle in the chicken stock, stirring continuously with the wooden spoon and making sure rice does not stick to the bottom of the pan. Add more stock as it is absorbed. For al dente rice, cook for 10 minutes and then stir in the asparagus sauce. Cook for 2 minutes longer for flavors to combine. (For less al dente rice, cook for 13 minutes then add sauce and cook 2 minutes longer).

Remove from heat and stir in the butter. Add pecorino cheese and salt to taste; stir well to incorporate. Let rest for a few minutes before serving.

7 cups chicken stock

4 tablespoons extra virgin olive oil

2 medium shallots, finely chopped

1 bunch (about 1½ pounds) wild asparagus (or very thin asparagus), diagonally cut into ½-inch pieces

1 tablespoon finely chopped flat leaf parsley

2 cups Sardinian Roma rice (see page 153)

¼ cup Vermentino wine (or other dry white wine)

4 tablespoons (½ stick) unsalted butter

1 cup grated Pecorino Sardo semi-stagionato cheese (or other semi-aged pecorino cheese)

Sea salt (preferably freshly ground)

Risotto with goat cheese and abbamele
Rosu Cremosu kin Abbathu
SERVES 4

This risotto combines the best of old and new—what I remember my mother making for us, and what I like to make today. It uses creamy goat cheese, young pecorino, and heavy cream to produce a very decadent white risotto enhanced by a sweet drizzle of abbamele. My mother was never so "over the top" with the cheese and cream, but she would appreciate the way the ancient ingredients combine to make a dish so rich you could mistake it for dessert.

◇　◇　◇

In a medium saucepan over high heat, bring the vegetable stock to a boil. Reduce heat to low, keeping stock hot.

In a thick-bottomed saucepan (copper is recommended), heat butter over medium-high heat. Add shallots and cook until translucent. Add the rice, stirring continuously with a wooden spoon for 2 to 3 minutes. Add the sparkling white wine, stirring until liquid is absorbed.

Gradually ladle in the vegetable stock and season to taste, stirring continuously with the wooden spoon, making sure rice does not stick to the bottom of the pan. Add more stock as it is absorbed for 12 minutes.

4 cups vegetable stock
4 tablespoons (½ stick) unsalted butter
1 shallot, minced
2 cups Sardinian Roma rice (see page 153)
½ cup sparkling white wine
½ cup creamy goat cheese
½ cup heavy cream
4 tablespoons abbamele (see page 59)
½ cup grated young Pecorino Sardo cheese
    (or other young pecorino cheese)
1 bunch chives, finely chopped

Stir in goat cheese and heavy cream until well incorporated. Add 2 tablespoons of abbamele and stir continuously for 3 to 5 minutes, until rice is creamy and al dente.

Remove from heat and stir in the pecorino and the chives. Drizzle with the remaining 2 tablespoons of abbamele before serving.

NURAGHI

When I drive through the mountains from Orosei to the rice fields near Oristano, my eyes always turn to the hills. There, among the fields filled with sheep and shepherds who produce our legendary pecorino, I look for the superb examples of the island's unique and most famous ancient ruins: the round towers called Nuraghi. Built by the Nuragic people between 1500 and 800 BC and made from basalt (volcanic rocks), these structures remain the subject of study and wonder. What were they? The ones high in the hills were used for communication. Others may have served as fortresses, places of worship, tombs, homes, or castles. Some feature multiple levels, hidden compartments, and connected rooms. What is certain is more than 7,000 are scattered and preserved across the island, including several in Orosei. The most elaborate can be found in the Su Nuraxi village on the edge of Barumini.

Risotto with cuttlefish ink and cuttlefish
Rosu Nieddu de Seppia

SERVES 4

When Zio Pietro took me harpooning, we hunted for cuttlefish along the rocks. But unlike grouper or the other white fish we caught, cuttlefish couldn't be speared; instead we had to take it in with a net. The trick was to avoid breaking the sack that held its wonderful ink, perfect for coloring pasta and risotto. Our reward would be this traditional Sardinian dish, based on a classic Catalan preparation.

◇   ◇   ◇

Clean cuttlefish thoroughly and remove bone, eyes, and beak. If necessary, remove outer skin. Rinse tentacles especially well to remove sand and other impurities. Cut cuttlefish into 1-inch (bite-size) pieces.

In a medium saucepan over high heat, bring the fish stock to a boil. Reduce heat to low, keeping stock hot.

In a medium saucepan, heat ¼ cup of the extra virgin olive oil over medium-high heat. Add garlic and green onion and cook for 2 minutes. Add cuttlefish and cook for 5 minutes. Pour in ½ cup of the wine and let alcohol evaporate. Stir in the tomato puree and pepperoncino. Add ¼ cup of the fish stock, cuttlefish ink, thyme, bay leaves, and parsley. Simmer for 10 minutes, stirring frequently to prevent sticking.

In a thick-bottomed saucepan (copper is best), heat 2 tablespoons of extra virgin olive oil over medium-high heat. Add shallot and cook until translucent. Add the rice, stirring continuously with a wooden spoon for 2 to 3 minutes. Add the remaining wine; simmer until liquid is absorbed.

Gradually ladle in the remaining fish stock and season to taste, stirring continuously with the wooden spoon to make sure rice does not stick to the bottom of the pan. Add more stock as it is absorbed for 12 minutes.

Add sauce to the rice and stir well. Let simmer for 3 to 5 minutes, stirring continuously. Remove from heat and add chives and remaining extra virgin olive oil, stirring well to combine.

6 medium cuttlefish
4 cups fish stock (see recipe, page 68)
½ cup extra virgin olive oil
1 garlic clove, minced
1 extra large green onion, chopped
1 cup Vermentino wine (or other dry white wine)
¼ cup tomato puree
1 fresh pepperoncino, chopped (or ½ teaspoon crushed red pepper)
½ tablespoon cuttlefish ink (or squid ink)
4 sprigs thyme, leaves only
2 bay leaves
1 bunch parsley, chopped
1 shallot, minced
2 cups Carnaroli rice (see page 153)
2 tablespoons finely chopped chives

Risotto with mussels, saffron, and bottarga
Rosu kin Cozzas Taffaranu e Buttariga

SERVES 4

This risotto is similar to ones you find in homes and restaurants in Olbia and Cagliari, cities where mussels are most abundant. But when I decided to include this recipe, I admit I was thinking of risotto Milanese, one of the most famous rice dishes in the world, which features saffron as a key ingredient. I wanted to include a Sardinian risotto that used saffron but did not want one that simply substituted pecorino for the Parmesan in Milanese. Then, I thought of Olbia and my father, who loves mussels and saffron. The combination of ingredients is strong, so use a delicate fish stock and the superfine Carnaroli rice to absorb it.

◇ ◇ ◇

Rinse mussels thoroughly to remove impurities.

In a medium saucepan over high heat, bring the fish stock to a boil. Reduce heat to low, keeping stock hot.

Heat 2 tablespoons of olive oil in a skillet over medium heat. Gently crack garlic cloves with the side of a knife and add to skillet to flavor the oil. Add mussels and cover for 3 to 4 minutes, until mussels begin to open. Add ½ cup of the wine and cook until alcohol evaporates. Add ½ cup of fish stock, the parsley, and saffron and let simmer for 3 minutes. Reserve 16 mussels and set aside; shell remaining mussels and return to pan. Remove garlic and discard.

In a thick-bottomed saucepan (copper is best), heat remaining 2 tablespoons of olive oil over medium-high heat. Add shallot and cook until translucent. Add the rice, stirring continuously with a wooden spoon for 2 to 3 minutes. Add remaining wine, stirring until alcohol is evaporated.

Gradually ladle in the fish stock, stirring continuously with the wooden spoon, making sure rice does not stick to the bottom of the pan. Add more stock as it is absorbed, until rice is al dente and creamy, for about 15 minutes. Add mussel sauce and stir until combined.

Remove from heat and stir in the grated bottarga. Add butter and stir until combined well. Let rest for a few minutes before serving, decorated with reserved mussels and shavings of bottarga.

3 pounds mussels

4 cups fish stock (see recipe, page 68)

4 tablespoons extra virgin olive oil

4 garlic cloves

1 cup Vermentino wine (or other dry white wine)

1 small bunch flat leaf parsley, finely chopped

Pinch of saffron

1 medium shallot, finely chopped

2 cups Carnaroli rice (see page 153)

2 tablespoons grated bottarga di muggine (see page 30)

4 tablespoons (½ stick) unsalted butter

1 ounce whole bottarga di muggine (see page 30), thinly shaved

ROMA AND CARNAROLI RICE

The first risotto recipes I offer in this book are classic Sardinian preparations and use the more common Roma rice. Short-grain Roma is terrific everyday rice for risottos and other rice dishes. Because of its appeal to home cooks, larger areas and resources are dedicated to the cultivation of Roma rice than to superfine long-grain Carnaroli rice. I use Carnaroli rice for my seafood risottos because of its perfect, creamy consistency. Carnaroli rice, which is grown in both Sardinia and Piedmont (a true legacy of the Kingdom of Sardinia), is renowned by chefs for more refined risottos such as ones with seafood and the rare white truffle.

Main Courses
Prattos Fortes

◈

Non bat mai mortu nessunu!

"Anything that doesn't kill you can feed you!"

Prattos fortes literally translates to "strong plate" in Sardo and, combined with the quote above, that pretty much says it all: We eat everything and we like that "everything" robust and hearty. We enjoy our *petha* (meat) but savor every other part of the animal, too. There are few varieties of *piske* (fish and shellfish) we will not try. Chicken, eggs–even our vegetables–are filling enough to eat as a meal. This is our soul food, the heart of Sardinian cuisine, and I can only begin to capture here what these dishes mean to my family, the island, and me. Eat your way through the few recipes I am able to present here, and I guarantee you'll be speaking Sardo by the time you're done.

Roasted pork belly
Sumene Arrustu
SERVES 4

The slaughter of a pig was an early winter ritual that brought my family and friends together for a couple of days of butchering and sharing of meat and more. The killing took place in the courtyard at my grandparents' house. After the blood was drained, we burned off the hair with torches of coarse fragrant elicriso (curry plant, or uscratina in Sardo), which filled the air with a currylike smell and cooked the skin just slightly. Once the pig was blackened (not burned) from the fire and flavored slightly from the elicriso, we hosed it down and scrubbed it with pumice stone to make it clean and white and ready for moving into the cucina rustica for butchering. That evening we divided the belly, setting aside some for my father to cure for pancetta and roasting the rest by the fire for this sweet and salty dish.

◇ ◇ ◇

Cut pork belly into 1½-inch strips. Toss with olive oil, salt, and pepper. Place strips in a baking dish, alternating with the fresh bay leaves. Cover and refrigerate for at least 2 hours.

Prepare grill to low heat. Place slices on the heated grill and cook for 4 minutes on each side. Brush cooked sides evenly with the mosto d'uva and cook for another minute.

Serve over sheets of pane carasau.

1½ pounds pork belly (preferably skin on)
2 tablespoons extra virgin olive oil
2 teaspoons sea salt
1 teaspoon freshly ground black pepper
16 to 20 fresh bay leaves
2 tablespoons mosto d'uva (see page 42)
4 sheets pane carasau (see page 22)

SAMBENEDDU

When I describe the killing of a pig to people who know nothing of slaughtering animals and prefer to think of meat magically appearing in the supermarket, they think it sounds terrible—but nothing connects you more to the animal. Mannai Carta used to tell me that a mouse would always tell a pig when it was about to be killed and that was why the pig seemed sad before the slaughter. In fact, we were sad before the slaughter, too. This was an animal we had nurtured for months to reach this end, but to see it go was still not easy. The slaughter was simply the final step in our lifelong connection to it. Thus nothing could be more disrespectful than to waste any of it; every bit was used for something—snout to foot.

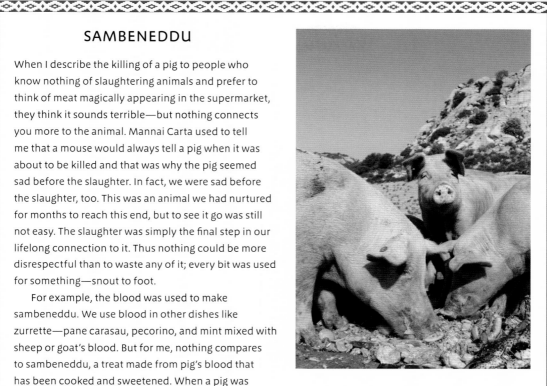

For example, the blood was used to make sambeneddu. We use blood in other dishes like zurrette—pane carasau, pecorino, and mint mixed with sheep or goat's blood. But for me, nothing compares to sambeneddu, a treat made from pig's blood that has been cooked and sweetened. When a pig was slaughtered, I was responsible for preserving the blood in a bucket and turning it constantly so it did not coagulate before we mixed it with mosto d'uva, vino cotto, sugar, cloves, and other aromatic herbs and spices. We then stuffed the mixture into the pig's intestines, which were tied off, boiled, and allowed to cool down before we gobbled up the insides—a deliciously sweet and wonderfully bloody treat no child (or adult) could resist.

Pork ribs with lentils and saba
Costillias de Porcu kin Lentizza e Sapa
SERVES 4

The slaughter of a pig was a time of celebration, joining friends and family around one of our most primal connections to life and death. Our pig, of course, was not the only pig in town, but one of many that linked friends and family throughout the late fall and early winter. It would take two days to complete the butchering, with the second day reserved for sectioning the carcass and cutting the meat for sausage. The host family would then thank the friends who helped by presenting them with s'ispinu—three of the ribs with the loin attached. The remaining ribs were cut from the loin, and our family ate them one at a time over the next couple of days. You will obviously serve your family more than one today, but you can celebrate the same way we did with this recipe of ribs and lentils, which, along with the juniper, make a fantastic combination.

◇   ◇   ◇

Soak lentils in fresh water at least 4 hours. Drain.

In a saucepan, warm beef stock over medium heat.

In a Dutch oven, heat olive oil over medium heat. Add ribs and sear on all sides. Pour in wine and let simmer a few minutes, stirring to release browned bits on the bottom of the pan. Stir in onion, garlic, thyme, rosemary, and juniper berries. Let cook for 5 minutes, stirring often. Stir in 1 cup of warm stock. Reduce heat to medium-low and cook, uncovered, for 20 minutes.

Stir in lentils and remaining 4 cups of stock. Season to taste with salt and pepper. Reduce heat to low and cook for 45 minutes.

Add saba, stir well to incorporate, and simmer for 5 minutes. Remove from heat and let rest a few minutes before serving. Serve with ribs atop a bed of the lentils.

1 pound French green lentils

5 cups beef stock

4 tablespoons extra virgin olive oil

2 pounds pork ribs, cut into 1-rib pieces

½ cup Cannonau wine (or other dry red wine)

1 medium onion, julienned

3 garlic cloves, cracked

6 sprigs thyme, leaves only

2 sprigs rosemary

6 juniper berries, smashed and finely chopped

Sea salt and freshly ground black pepper

⅓ cup saba (see page 42)

ELICRISO AND JUNIPER

Elicriso and juniper, which are linked through the slaughter of the pig, also grow together on the coast of Sardinia. Both are hearty plants that stand up to the sea. You may not have heard of elicriso, an evergreen that loves our sandy shores. The leaves have the mild flavor of curry (its English name is "curry plant") and it can be used as an herb in sweet or savory foods. Juniper may be familiar to you as berries used in distilling gin. In Sardinia, we use the same berries to flavor a variety of dishes, especially pork meat. But we also used the wood to build, and the resulting over-cutting almost led to its demise. Today, the berries are as popular as ever, but the branches are protected by the state.

Polenta with sausage and tomato sauce
Pulenta kin Sartizza

SERVES 4

A*t the time of the slaughter of a pig, the men worked around the table butchering the pig, while the women and children took pieces of meat and some fat and placed it in the* lacu, *a shallow trough, to be chopped together with salt, herbs, garlic, vinegar, and maybe some red wine to make sausage. The seasoned meat would marinate before being cranked through a sausage stuffer and into the natural casing. The filled casings were tied off and turned and rolled into a curved shape. We hung the fresh sausage pieces on a piece of bamboo laid across two chairs, where it dried overnight. The next day we moved the sausage by the fireplace, where it was warm and dry. (In old houses, you still see hooks by the fireplace for hanging sausage.) After a month or so, it was ready—the familiar, thin-sliced sausage like you see in an antipasti. But before then, my mother would pull down a small piece for this dish. With the sausage still "fresh," she roasted it by the fire and sliced it thickly for use in this casserole-like dish, adding her own preserved tomato sauce and grain we had stored for winter.*

◊ ◊ ◊

Roast the sausage in a 400°F oven until brown, turning once. Slice sausage in ¼-inch slices.

In a medium skillet, heat 2 tablespoons of olive oil over medium heat. Add onion and sauté until golden brown. Add sliced sausage and brown.

Add the wine and deglaze, scraping browned bits from bottom of pan. Stir in tomato sauce and reduce heat to a simmer, stirring often.

In a large stockpot, bring 5 cups of water to a boil; add polenta gradually. Stir continuously with a whisk until mixture is creamy, about 2 minutes. Season with salt to taste.

Preheat oven to 350°F.

In a 2-quart baking dish, layer half of the polenta and top with half of the sausage and tomato sauce mixture. Sprinkle with half of the grated pecorino. Repeat with the remaining polenta, then sauce and pecorino.

Finish in preheated oven for 10 minutes. Serve sprinkled with basil and drizzle with remaining tablespoon of olive oil.

1 pound fresh mild Italian sausage
3 tablespoons extra virgin olive oil
1 medium onion, finely chopped
½ cup of Vermentino wine (or other dry white wine)
2 cups tomato sauce (see recipe, page 92)
2 cups polenta
Sea salt
1 cup grated Pecorino Sardo cheese (or other pecorino cheese)
1 bunch basil, finely chopped

Pork tenderloin with saba glaze
Porcu a sa Sapa

SERVES 4

*T*oday *in Orosei, pigs are rarely killed and butchered at home. Though we still demand good, fresh pork meat and want to know where it comes from, we have more slaughterhouses and butchers. And today, we can go to the butcher and ask for pork tenderloin or a roast—when we butchered the pig ourselves, to eat the tenderloin alone would be extravagant. Instead, except for the piece given to friends as a thank you for helping with the butchering, we stretched the loin by chopping it and mixing it with the fat to make sausage. This recipe of my sister Angela's is perfect for the tenderloin we now serve. The Mediterranean herbs and saba combine to give a deep traditional flavor to this "modern" cut.*

◇   ◇   ◇

Place tenderloin in a baking dish. Prepare the marinade by mixing ½ cup of olive oil, 2 tablespoons of saba, garlic, thyme, rosemary, and bay leaf. Pour marinade over the tenderloin and cover. Refrigerate overnight (at least 8 hours), turning at least once.

In a roasting pan, heat remaining 2 tablespoons of olive oil over high heat. Place tenderloin in the roasting pan and sear all sides evenly, reserving marinade.

Preheat oven to 350°F.

Add the wine and deglaze the pan. Stir in the reserved marinade and vegetable stock. Place in preheated oven and cook for 20 to 25 minutes, turning once, or until almost cooked through.

Set tenderloin aside. Strain cooking liquids; discard herbs. Pour liquid into a medium skillet. In a small bowl, dissolve cornstarch in 2 tablespoons of water; add to skillet. Stir in ¼ cup of the saba. Bring sauce to a boil then reduce heat, stirring often until sauce thickens. Season to taste and set aside, keeping warm.

Return tenderloin to roasting pan and brush with 2 tablespoons of saba. Place under the broiler for 2 minutes. Turn and brush other side with the remaining 2 tablespoons of saba and broil for 2 minutes longer until saba caramelizes.

Slice tenderloin and serve with the saba sauce.

1½ pounds pork tenderloin, trimmed

½ cup plus 2 tablespoons extra virgin olive oil

2 tablespoons plus ½ cup saba (see page 42)

2 garlic cloves, minced

8 sprigs thyme

4 sprigs rosemary

1 bay leaf

1 cup Terra Saliosa wine (or other dry red wine)

1 cup vegetable stock

1 teaspoon cornstarch

Sea salt and freshly ground black pepper

Sardinian suckling pig
Porkeddu a sa Baroniesa

SERVES 4

Suckling pig is one of our most renowned culinary traditions and the centerpiece of our most important celebrations. I first remember seeing it after the wedding of a cousin. Returning from the church, we were greeted by a mesmerizing row of suckling pigs slow-roasting on aromatic spits of wood in front of an open fire. The pigs were only forty days old, just weaned, and weighed only fifteen to eighteen pounds. They had come from a specially selected farm and had been raised and slaughtered expressly to celebrate the marriage. The pigs were prepared that morning by an expert s'arrostitore like Zio Valerio, who stoked the fire and turned the spits for a solid five hours, brushing the pigs with their own blood, myrtle leaves, and hot lard. If you have a good spit, an open fire, access to whole suckling pig, and an occasion to celebrate, perhaps you can try our traditional method. If you can find pieces of suckling pig with skin on (or a similar cut of lamb or goat), try this recipe on your stovetop.

◇　◇　◇

In a large thick-bottomed stockpot, heat 2 tablespoons of olive oil over medium-high heat. Cook the carrots, celery, onion, garlic, and bay leaves for 8 to 10 minutes, until softened, stirring continuously with a wooden spoon.

In a large pot, heat the remaining 2 tablespoons olive oil over high heat. Add the suckling pig pieces, turning gently with the wooden spoon and searing all sides. Incorporate the wine, stirring continuously to deglaze and scraping browned bits from bottom of pan.

Reduce heat to medium; add cooked vegetables. Cover with hot water (about 2 cups) and season with salt. Cover and cook for 1 hour. Uncover and cook 1 hour longer.

Gently stir in the black olives and thyme and cook for another 10 minutes or until most of the liquid is a thick gravy. Let rest before serving.

4 tablespoons extra virgin olive oil

2 medium carrots, diced

2 stalks celery, diced

1 medium white onion, diced

3 garlic cloves, minced

2 bay leaves

3 pounds suckling pig, skin on and bones in, cut into 12 pieces

1 cup Cannonau wine (or other dry red wine)

1 teaspoon sea salt

1 cup Bosana black olives (or Niçoise or Kalamata)

2 sprigs thyme

THE SPIT

Roasting meats on a spit is not reserved for cooking a suckling pig and celebrations; it is the most traditional way to cook lamb, wild boar, or goat in Sardinia. Even today, it is not unusual to visit a shepherd like my friend Mattiu and see spits made from different types of wood stacked along the side of the house. During one of my visits, I could still smell cooked meat on one of the spits, which reminded me of Zio Valerio. He taught me the art of spitting. Whenever we walked to see one of his shepherd friends, my uncle inevitably spotted a perfect branch of olive, oak, or myrtle. "Look at this!" he would exclaim as he cut it down and sized it up like the barrel of a gun. "Beautiful." It always was. And so was he.

Suckling pig with myrtle
Porkeddu kin Murta
SERVES 4

In the old days, when one of your pigs went missing, you might ask a group of gentlemen sitting nearby whether they had seen one pass by. No, it had not passed, they would reply. It was cooking in the ground beneath them! If Porkeddu a sa Baroniesa is the most traditional and widespread way to serve suckling pig in Sardinia, this method is a bit more underground. Literally. Pig rustlers may have used this preparation, but its origin is a practical and ingenious shepherd technique for roasting meat and infusing it with the sweet perfume of myrtle. First, you dig a hole and light a fire in it to heat the earth and stones beneath. Then, remove the hot coals, put in the suckling pig wrapped in the sweet perfume of myrtle branches, and cover with the coals. Finally, refill the hole and wait four hours to dig it up and savor a dish that is truly from the land. If you have a shovel, a place to dig, can build a fire, and have access to whole suckling pig, you can use this method, too. If you can find pieces of suckling pig with skin on, try this similar recipe in your oven.

◊　◊　◊

Place some of the myrtle leaves in the bottom of a baking dish. Place the suckling pig, skin side down, on top of the myrtle leaves. Top with the garlic and more myrtle leaves. Drizzle with olive oil, cover, and refrigerate overnight (at least 8 hours).

Preheat oven to 375°F.

Place rock salt in the bottom of a large roasting pan. Place myrtle leaves and garlic on top of the rock salt. Lay the suckling pig skin side up on the myrtle leaves and sprinkle with the sea salt. Tuck remaining myrtle leaves on top and around the suckling pig. Cover with aluminum foil and bake for 3 hours.

Remove roasting pan from oven and turn broiler on. Uncover suckling pig and remove myrtle leaves. Coat skin with additional olive oil and place under broiler for 3 minutes to give the suckling pig color and crispness.

1 large bunch myrtle (see page 23), about 3 to 4 branches

3 pounds suckling pig, skin on and bones in

6 garlic cloves, cracked and halved

2 to 3 tablespoons extra virgin olive oil, plus more for coating

2 pounds rock salt

1 tablespoon sea salt

FILU'E FERRU

Filu'e Ferru is a traditional Sardinian distillate made from the remaining grape skin and flesh after the grapes have been pressed for wine. *Filu'e ferru* means "barbed wire" in Sardo, but how it is made is not as interesting as how it got its name. It was illegal to distill grappa without a license, but many people did anyway. And like my father, they used barbed wire to mark the ground where they had buried their stills. (The police could smell the grappa but never find it). My father made his in our garden, and I remember the smell was so strong it filled the streets near our home. My mother was sure our still would be discovered and begged him to stop. (In fact, the fumes once killed a mandarin orange tree in our yard, but the police never came.) Today, my friends in Berchidda at Lucrezio Distillery (see page 109) and others make grappa in bright, new, and legal facilities well above ground—but the name has stayed the same.

Red cow with porcini mushrooms
Filetto de su Voe Ruiu

SERVES 4

Recently, I went with my friend Pietro to visit friends behind the "red cow movement" in Seneghe in the Montiferru region. My grandfather had told me stories of encountering red cows when he traveled to barter for goods in the area. Since it was one of the last days of Carnevale, our friends invited us back to town for the evening celebration, and I was stunned by the festivities in the town square. The voices of a quartet and the notes of an accordion filled the air with ancient words and music, while women and men danced a promenade around them. My grandfather told me that traditional dances like these used to happen in small villages all over the area, and here I was watching it for the first time. This garlicky, woodsy, and hearty dish is a tribute to the people of Seneghe and the flavors of the land that surround their wonderful beast.

◇ ◇ ◇

In a saucepan over medium heat, heat 4 tablespoons of the olive oil and add thinly sliced garlic, cooking until softened. Add mushrooms and toss well, cooking for 3 minutes. Pour in the wine and cook until the liquids are absorbed. Stir in ½ cup of the demi-glace and salt to taste; simmer for 5 minutes.

Heat the remaining 2 tablespoons of olive oil in a large sauté pan over medium-high heat. Add the 2 cracked garlic cloves, thyme, rosemary, myrtle, and juniper berries; cook for 2 minutes to flavor the oil. Sear both sides of the fillets. Add mosto d'uva and deglaze the pan.

Reduce heat to medium and add the remaining demi-glace to the pan. Cook for 4 minutes. Stir in parsley, turn fillets, and cook 4 minutes longer for a medium to medium-rare cooking temperature. Discard garlic, rosemary, and myrtle.

Serve fillets topped with the mosto d'uva sauce and accompanied by the porcini mushrooms.

6 tablespoons extra virgin olive oil

6 garlic cloves (4 thinly sliced and 2 cracked)

1 pound porcini mushrooms

½ cup dry white wine

1½ cups demi-glace

Sea salt

6 sprigs of thyme, leaves only

1 sprig rosemary

1 sprig myrtle leaves (see page 23)

6 juniper berries, cracked

4 fillets Bue Rosso (or Black Angus), 6 ounces each, trimmed

¼ cup mosto d'uva (see page 42)

½ bunch flat leaf parsley, finely chopped

THE RED COW

Sardinia's Montiferru ("iron mountain") region is a rustic land of five-hundred-year-old basalt houses, ancient stone walls, and gnarled olive trees producing some of the island's finest olive oil. Here, grazing in the shade of the hillside olive groves, are the last of the region's prized heirloom animals: *il bue rosso* of the Sardo-Modicana breed—the red cow of Sardinia. One hundred and fifty years ago, this giant ox covered the mountain pastures. Enormously powerful, the red cow could tow a cart, work the land, and produce wonderful milk, cheese (our legendary casizzolu), and meat. It has been so valued over time, it has the honor of pulling the cart of Saint Efisio, the patron saint of Sardinia, during festivals. Then the machines came; tractors and cars replaced oxen all over the island, and the red cow fell out of favor for work and transportation. With alternative options for milk and meat, the animal soon became endangered, until a small group of townspeople stepped in to try and rescue it. Today, there are four thousand red cows in Montiferru and its meat is revered all over Italy.

Beef braised in red wine
Petha Imbinata
SERVES 4

This delicious dish "honors" a notorious (and legendary) aspect of the Sardinian past: our bandits. Today, Orgoloso, near Nuoro, is famous for dozens of magnificent modern murals that comment on everything from life in the Barbagia region to island politics. But until late in the last century, the region was home to sheep and cattle rustlers and other ruthless bandits. Despite nighttime patrols of cattlemen and vigilantes, the rustlers stole animals from the region almost at will. They sometimes managed to escape by cutting off the cow's legs and head and then hiding the torso in the wine barrels in the cellar. When the time came to move the valuable meat, they had not only aged it but unintentionally marinated it. This recipe knowingly does the same.

◇　◇　◇

Place meat in a large bowl. Add bay leaf, juniper berries, thyme, rosemary, and star anise. Pour the wine over herbs and beef. Cover and refrigerate overnight (at least 8 hours).

Remove meat from marinade, reserving marinade. Pat the meat dry. Sprinkle with salt and pepper.

In a saucepan, heat olive oil and garlic over medium-high heat. Add meat and brown evenly; stir in shallots. Add one ladleful of the marinade to the saucepan. Reduce heat to medium. Add remaining marinade and bring to a boil. Reduce heat to medium-low and simmer for 40 minutes.

Remove the meat to a hot plate and keep it warm. Pass marinade through a sieve lined with cheesecloth, returning liquid to saucepan. Combine cornstarch with 3 tablespoons cold water; stir until combined. Add cornstarch mixture and mosto d'uva to sauce. Bring to a boil, reduce heat, and simmer for 5 minutes. Pour sauce over meat before serving.

2 pounds beef top round, trimmed and cubed
2 bay leaves
1 tablespoon juniper berries, cracked
6 sprigs thyme
1 sprig rosemary
2 star anise
Sea salt and freshly ground black pepper
1 bottle (750 ml) dry red wine
4 tablespoons extra virgin olive oil
3 garlic cloves, cracked
3 shallots, minced
1 tablespoon cornstarch
⅓ cup mosto d'uva (see page 42)

Stuffed eggplant
Perdinzanu Prenu
SERVES 4

When I am homesick, I long for this dish: my mother's "Sardinian meatloaf." She made it for us every spring as soon as the first eggplants (called primizie or "first pick") came in. Her preparation was very precise, and she let us help only if we made it exactly as she told us, with every piece of eggplant scooped perfectly round. (We used an espresso spoon as you would a small melon baller.) I still make sure I do it her way, but you and your children can be a little less exact. If you or your family have never been fans of eggplant, try this dish. You can make almost all of it a day ahead. Just prep everything and refrigerate until you are ready to bake.

◇   ◇   ◇

2 eggplants (about 1 pound each), halved lengthwise

1 teaspoon sea salt, plus more to taste

2 cans (14.5 ounces each) peeled plum tomatoes, drained

4 tablespoons extra virgin olive oil

3 garlic cloves, chopped

1 medium white onion, finely chopped

2 bay leaves, crushed to a powder

½ cup dry white wine

½ pound ground veal

1 cup grated Pecorino Sardo cheese (or other pecorino cheese)

2 eggs, lightly beaten

½ cup plain bread crumbs

¼ teaspoon freshly grated nutmeg

2 sprigs basil, chopped

2 sprigs mint, chopped

Using a spoon, scoop the flesh from the eggplant halves, leaving a ½-inch-thick shell. Chop the scooped-out eggplant flesh and place it in a colander. Toss the chopped eggplant with 1 teaspoon of sea salt and let drain 30 minutes. Working in handfuls, squeeze out as much of the water as possible. (This should yield about 1½ cups of chopped eggplant.)

In a bowl, crush canned tomatoes with a food mill or fork, discarding any unripened pieces. Set ½ cup aside. In a medium skillet, heat 1 tablespoon of olive oil over medium heat. Add garlic and cook until golden, add tomatoes, and stir until thickened, about 10 minutes. Season with salt to taste. Set sauce aside.

In a large deep skillet, heat remaining 3 tablespoons of olive oil. Add the onion and bay leaves and cook over medium heat until the onion is softened, about 5 minutes. Add the chopped eggplant and cook, stirring occasionally, until tender and just beginning to brown, about 15 minutes. Add the wine and raise the temperature to medium-high; add the veal. Cook, stirring and breaking up the meat, until cooked through and lightly browned, about 5 minutes longer. Transfer the eggplant filling to a bowl and let cool.

Bring a large pot of salted water to a boil. Set a wire rack on a baking sheet. Add the 4 eggplant shells to the pot and cook, gently poking them under to keep submerged, until just tender, about 3 minutes. Using a slotted spoon, transfer the eggplant shells to the wire rack to drain and cool. Lightly oil a baking dish and arrange the eggplant shells cut sides up.

Stir ½ cup of the pecorino, eggs, bread crumbs, nutmeg, basil, mint, and reserved ½ cup of tomatoes into the eggplant filling. Spoon the filling into the eggplant shells. Preheat the oven to 350°F.

Spoon the sauce over the eggplants and sprinkle with the remaining ½ cup of grated pecorino. Bake until browned and bubbling, about 35 minutes. Let cool for 5 to 10 minutes before serving.

Tripe in tomato sauce
Busecca

SERVES 4

Nowadays our animals are brought to a central slaughterhouse, but in the past every butcher had his own slaughter room in the back of the store. He would kill the animals there a couple of times a week and then bring the meat to the front. Except for tripe; lowly tripe never made it to the counter. It stayed in the back until people specifically asked for it, and the butcher would hand it to them out the back door, uncleaned. But what a wonderful mess it was. I remember watching my aunts in my grandfather's house scrubbing it clean to make dishes like this one, and I have loved it ever since. Plus, making tripe nowadays is easier than it used to be—it comes clean and you don't need to find a butcher's back door. I love it in soups and recipes like this one, in which the texture and flavor blend perfectly with the pecorino and tomato. Serve it over some plain risotto or atop a bed of steamed rice.

◇   ◇   ◇

Boil tripe in salted water over medium-high heat for at least 30 minutes. Drain well and cut into strips. Set aside.

In a large saucepan, heat olive oil over medium heat. Add onion and cook until softened. Add tripe, celery, carrot, and bay leaf and cook for 5 minutes. Add tomatoes, bring to a boil and season to taste. Reduce heat to low and cook for 30 minutes, stirring frequently to prevent sticking.

Remove from heat and stir in mint and cheese.

2 pounds tripe (cleaned)
4 tablespoons extra virgin olive oil
½ yellow onion, minced
½ stalk celery
1 small carrot, halved
1 bay leaf
2 cans (14.5 ounces each) peeled plum
    tomatoes, undrained and chopped
1 sprig peppermint, leaves only, chopped
1 cup grated young Pecorino Sardo cheese
    (or other young pecorino cheese)

Calf liver and onions with Vernaccia
Icatu de Vitellu
SERVES 4

I did not grow up eating a lot of beef. We more often ate liver and tripe, which were less expensive and more filling. But we did not eat just any calf's liver. The quality and flavor of organ meat is closely linked to how the animal is raised. My mother, like my grandmother, insisted on knowing the liver's origin–to know whose calf was getting killed that week so she could trust the liver would be good. Sometimes she just grilled it to accompany pasta. I always preferred this modest dish of liver, onions, and wine that she learned from my grandmother.

◇ ◇ ◇

In a hot nonstick skillet, sear both sides of the liver for about 30 seconds per side. Cut into strips and set aside.

Heat olive oil in a saucepan over medium heat. Add onion and cook until softened. Add liver, bay leaf, sage, and season to taste; toss well for about 2 minutes. Add the wine and let simmer until sauce thickens.

Stir in parsley. Cook for 3 minutes.

2 pounds calf liver

4 tablespoons extra virgin olive oil

1 white onion, julienned

1 bay leaf

3 sprigs sage, leaves only

Sea salt and freshly ground black pepper

1 cup aged Vernaccia wine (or Malvasia wine)

½ bunch flat leaf parsley, chopped

Calf sweetbreads with wild fennel
Carresapida kin Inucru

SERVES 4

Tripe, liver, and now sweetbreads: by now you know, Sardinians eat the entire animal, be it a pig, goat, or cow, and I want you to taste as many animals as you can, inside and out. In this case, you also get to sample the essence of another flavor of the land: the delectable wild fennel that grows in the hills of Orosei and all over the island. Calf sweetbreads were less common than those from lamb, but when they appeared, I looked forward to eating this full, complex, and filling recipe.

◇   ◇   ◇

Add the white wine vinegar to a large pot of salted boiling water. Blanch the sweetbreads for 10 minutes. Remove and rinse under cold running water to cool; pat dry. Cut into strips, trimming further if necessary. Lightly dredge in flour, shake to remove any excess flour, and set aside.

Coat bottom of a Dutch oven with olive oil and heat over medium heat. Add sweetbreads and cook for 5 minutes, turning once. Pour in the wine and deglaze the pan. Stir in fennel, garlic, thyme, rosemary, and bay leaves; season with salt to taste. Let cook for 2 minutes for flavors to combine.

Add vegetable stock and parsley. Bring to a boil and add potatoes. Reduce heat to medium-low and let simmer for 25 minutes, stirring often, until potatoes are tender.

Serve vegetables and sweetbreads with the remaining cooking liquids, discarding whole herbs.

1 tablespoon white wine vinegar

2 pound calf sweetbreads, trimmed

¼ cup all-purpose flour

1 to 2 tablespoons extra virgin olive oil

½ cup dry white wine

2 bulbs fennel, cut into thin wedges

4 garlic cloves, cracked

6 sprigs thyme

1 sprig rosemary

2 bay leaves

Sea salt

2 cups vegetable stock

½ bunch flat leaf parsley, chopped

2 potatoes, peeled and cut into wedges

WILD FENNEL

My family has many uses for wild fennel (*finocchietto selvatico*). It flavors our dishes as in this recipe and is especially good with lamb. We also hang it in the cantina or the cellar to perfume the air. My father used it when he rinsed barrels, leaving behind a subtle aroma of anise. But wild fennel is not exactly the same as the cultivated fennel you find in America. While it has the consistency of fennel, the small bulb heads, stalks, and flavor are similar to dill, which I sometimes use in its place.

Lamb with new potatoes and artichokes
Anzone kin Patata e Carzofeddas

SERVES 4

This superb one-pot dish of my mother's captures the essence of what it means to eat seasonally in Sardinia. Even if she could find these ingredients in a supermarket in the fall, she would never think of making it then. This is a spring dish. The only substitutions might be another part of the lamb (like some meat and bones from the leg) or other seasonal produce like fennel or fava beans. But the most remarkable part of this dish is that it requires only water for its hearty broth. The water offers a neutral palette for the ingredients to combine as they cook.

In a large ceramic pot, heat olive oil. Add lamb and cook until browned. Add wine and deglaze, scraping browned bits from bottom of pan. Add garlic, parsley, bay leaf, rosemary, thyme, 1 teaspoon of sea salt, and pearl onions. Let roast over medium heat for 5 minutes.

Stir in potatoes and artichokes. Gently toss to combine flavors, about 3 minutes. Add hot water to cover (about 4 cups) and remaining sea salt. Cook uncovered for 40 to 45 minutes, gently stirring occasionally, until lamb is tender.

¼ cup extra virgin olive oil

2 to 3 pounds lamb loin chops (or cubed lamb shoulder)

½ cup Vermentino wine (or other dry white wine)

4 garlic cloves, crushed

1 bunch flat leaf parsley, torn

1 bay leaf

1 sprig rosemary

2 sprigs thyme

2 teaspoons sea salt

12 pearl onions

½ pound new potatoes, halved

4 artichokes, quartered and cleaned (see page 34)

THE PRIVATE SIDE OF SA SARTIGLIA

Sometimes it is what you do not see that makes a public spectacle like Oristano's magnificent Carnevale celebration, Sa Sartiglia, even more special. For a look at the public face of Sa Sartiglia, see the sidebar on page 237. What ends as an incredible event and riding competition awash in history and witnessed by thousands begins as an intimate spread for family and friends of the riders. What made it special for me was when my friend Giorgio (one of the riders in the competition) invited me to join him there that morning to enjoy a spread of grilled meat and bread, drink wine, hear tales of previous years, and watch "La Vestitura," or the dressing of the riders and the horses.

When the riders put on the traditional white masks, you can feel the spirit of centuries of tradition run through the crowd. Everyone stands in quiet awe as they ride off to join other stables in the procession into town, glasses of Vernaccia di Oristano—the spicy amber wine that is a specialty of the region—raised in salute to the team and the tradition. The evening after Sa Sartiglia brings more celebrating with guests who pack long tables for a meal that might include such seasonal specialties as lamb with artichokes and new potatoes, *nervetti* (cooked pig cartilage), a simple pasta dish like malloreddus and tomato sauce, the sweets of Carnevale, and more glasses of wine.

Sardinian simmered goat
Crapittu a Sarza

SERVES 4

I have always had a tender spot for goats: the colors of their fur, their bearded baby faces. I love watching the shepherds send them into the mountains after their milking (the lambs got the pastures; the goats would eat your trees). In Sardinia, goats are raised largely for milk and cheese, so goat meat is much rarer than pig or lamb—in our home it would usually be reserved for my grandfather to barter with or for us to eat just like suckling pig at special occasions or celebrations. This traditional recipe comes from Zia Maria, who learned it from her mother-in-law, Zia Rosedda.

◇   ◇   ◇

In a large saucepan, heat olive oil over medium-high heat. Roast the goat until browned evenly on all sides. Pour in the wine and simmer for 5 minutes. Stir in onion and season to taste. Reduce heat to medium.

Add 3 cups of warm water (making sure meat is mostly covered). Bring to a boil, then reduce heat to medium-low and stir in parsley. Cook uncovered for 1 hour, until liquid is reduced. Stir often to turn meat and to avoid sticking.

In a small bowl, whisk eggs with the lemon juice. Remove stew from heat and add the egg mixture, stirring continuously until sauce becomes creamy. Serve hot.

4 tablespoons extra virgin olive oil

2 pounds goat (or lamb), trimmed, cut into 2- to 3-inch pieces

½ cup Vermentino wine (or other dry white wine)

½ medium yellow onion, minced

Sea salt and freshly ground black pepper

½ bunch flat leaf parsley, finely chopped

3 eggs

Juice of 1 lemon

CORDEDDA AND TATTALIU

While we usually eat the fresh and seasonal, I must admit freezers are good for at least one thing: if I cannot come home in the spring, my mother can still save me cordedda (braided lamb intestine) or tattaliu (braided goat intestine and organs) for my next visit.

Zio Valerio is one of the expert butchers in town (see page 75), and he always brought us all the entrails and organs after the slaughter. My mother would then start the intricate and beautiful process of creating this cordedda, which required one or more lamb intestines to make, as the long thin parts were braided around the fatty end and stomach. Today, we reserve cordedda from the butcher months in advance but eat it the same way: roasted in the oven or on a spit in front of the fire with potatoes, green peas, and rosemary. Tattaliu is similar to cordedda except the middle is filled with the goat's organs and a little pork belly to add some fat (organs are very lean). All the organs are used except the stomach, which the shepherd would have filled with the goat's milk and hung inside the cucina rustica, the acid of the stomach transforming into a coagulant used to make cheese. Tattaliu is also cooked exclusively on a spit rotated in front of an open fire, not in the oven.

Wild boar with red wine and saba
Sirvone Acru-Durke

SERVES 4

Sardinians have hunted wild boar for thousands of years, and today it remains a staple of our cuisine. Living near the coast, my family was not made up of hunters like families farther inland, but many townspeople hunted the boar that thrived in the mountains in and around Orosei (for deer, you had to travel farther). On Sundays during the winter, the children would often sit by the side of the main road and wait for the hunters to come down from the hills with their carts full with the day's kills. A friend of the family would always extend a taste for me and my family to take home. With wild boar becoming more widely available in the United States, I urge you to try it too. This sweet and savory recipe comes from my sister Angela, whose husband Giulio grew up hunting in the mountains of Nuoro.

◇　◇　◇

Place pieces of wild boar in a baking dish. Add 2 tablespoons of the saba, the wine, juniper berries, rosemary, bay leaves, sage, thyme, and garlic. Cover and refrigerate overnight (at least 8 hours).

In a large saucepan, heat olive oil over medium heat. Add onion and cook until softened. Add carrot, celery, and shallots and cook for 5 minutes, stirring frequently.

Remove wild boar from marinade, reserving marinade. Place wild boar in saucepan with vegetables and brown all sides evenly. Add the vinegar and stir for 1 minute. Add marinade and salt to saucepan, stirring occasionally to prevent sticking. Let simmer for 2 hours.

Place wild boar on a hot platter and keep it warm. Strain cooking liquids and return to saucepan. Dissolve the cornstarch in 1 tablespoon warm water and stir in to sauce. Add remaining saba. Boil 1 minute to thicken the sauce. Serve wild boar topped with the sauce.

2 pounds wild boar, trimmed and cut into 10 to 12 pieces

4 tablespoons saba (see page 42)

1 bottle (750 ml) dry red wine

10 juniper berries, cracked

3 sprigs rosemary

3 bay leaves

3 sprigs sage

5 sprigs thyme

4 garlic cloves, cracked

2 tablespoons extra virgin olive oil

1 medium onion, diced

2 medium carrots, diced

3 stalks celery, diced

2 shallots, diced

2 tablespoons red wine vinegar

1 teaspoon sea salt

1 teaspoon cornstarch

Whole sea bass with rosemary and potatoes
Ispigola kin Ramasinu
SERVES 4

The beauty of Zia Maria's restaurant, Su Barchile, belies its humble origins as a small pagoda that served drinks and snacks during the summer on the beach in the northern part of Orosei. At first, the pagoda was just a bar with three tables that often attracted fishermen. My brother Salvatore, my sisters Angela and Teresa, and I used to serve them and help clean whatever they caught—octopus, grouper, sea bass. Eventually, people on the beach saw us cleaning the fish and, knowing it could not be fresher, took it away to cook it. So, my aunt decided to cook some too—just simple dishes like soup, seafood salad, or a whole grilled fish like this recipe. Soon people came up to her and instead of buying the fresh fish asked, "Hey, what are you making today?" My aunt always offered them a plate. Of course, she never asked for money, but they gave her some anyway and kept coming back. Three years later, she and Pietro closed the pagoda and opened her restaurant in the center of Orosei, where it still thrives more than three decades later.

◇   ◇   ◇

Rinse the bass under running water, making sure all scales are removed.

Preheat oven to 400°F.

In a bowl, toss the potatoes with 2 tablespoons of olive oil. Add the leaves from 4 of the rosemary sprigs and season with salt and black pepper. Toss well to coat evenly. Set aside.

Coat the bottom of a large roasting pan with 2 tablespoons of the olive oil. Place remaining sprigs of rosemary and the garlic inside the fish. Place the fish in the pan. Drizzle with remaining 2 tablespoons of olive oil. Sprinkle with sea salt. Arrange potatoes around fish and place in preheated oven. Cook for 30 minutes.

Pour the wine over the fish. Stir the potatoes, then add hot fish stock. Return the pan to the oven and cook until the potatoes are tender, about 25 minutes.

Debone fish: With the fish lying flat, first make a cut along the spine from head to tail. Then, make a cut on the stomach side from head to tail. Insert your knife at the head and cut horizontally, carefully freeing the fillet from the bones in the center. Carefully pull the spine and all bones away and discard.

Slice each fillet in half and serve accompanied by potatoes and drizzled with the cooking liquids.

1 whole sea bass (about 4 pounds), cleaned
1 pound new potatoes, peeled
6 tablespoons extra virgin olive oil
6 sprigs rosemary
1 teaspoon sea salt
1 teaspoon freshly ground black pepper
3 garlic cloves, crushed
1 cup Vermentino wine (or other dry white wine)
1 cup fish stock (see recipe, page 68), hot

Whole grouper in tomato sauce
Cernia in Umidu

SERVES 4

While Zia Maria ran the pagoda, Zio Pietro went harpooning for sea bass and grouper. My uncle's passion for the sea was so strong he used to act like a fish, pretending he had fins and diving under the water. It made him feel connected to his prey. The imitation was a sign of respect and gratitude. He caught the grouper in the small caves on the shore where it would hide. He cleaned it by the shore, tossing the remains back into the sea to feed the fish he left behind. He then brought the whole fish back to the pagoda where my aunt would make us this one-pot dish using fresh tomatoes from our garden.

◊ ◊ ◊

Rinse the grouper under running water, making sure all scales are removed. Pat fish dry.

In a large saucepan, heat olive oil over medium heat. Add onions and cook until softened. Add pepperoncini and garlic, pour in the wine, and simmer for 2 minutes. Add tomatoes and salt to taste. Stir in parsley and fennel, then bring to a boil. Reduce heat to medium-low and cook for 15 minutes.

Preheat oven to 350°F. Pour the tomato sauce into a baking dish and place fish on top of sauce. Sprinkle fish with a pinch of sea salt. Cover with foil and bake until the fish flakes apart easily when prodded gently with the tip of a knife, about 45 minutes, turning fish once halfway.

Debone fish: With the fish lying flat, first make a cut along the spine from head to tail. Then, make a cut on the stomach side from head to tail. Insert your knife at the head and cut horizontally, carefully freeing the fillet from the bones in the center. Carefully pull the spine and all bones away and discard.

Cut the fillets in half and serve with sauce.

2 whole grouper (about 2 pounds each), cleaned

6 tablespoons extra virgin olive oil

1 bunch green onions, chopped

2 fresh pepperoncini, chopped (or 1 to 2 tablespoons crushed red pepper)

2 garlic cloves, minced

½ cup Vermentino wine (or other dry white wine)

3 cans (14.5 ounces each) peeled plum tomatoes, undrained and chopped

Sea salt

1 bunch flat leaf parsley, finely chopped

1 bunch fennel (preferably wild), chopped

Saragu with herbs and capers
Saragu in Umidu

SERVES 4

My sister Teresa went to university in the city of Cagliari, and whenever I visited, we always bought our lunch at San Benedetto, one of the greatest and most beautiful fish markets in the Mediterranean. Then, and even more importantly today, when buying fish there I always look for signs that say "Mare Sardo" (from the sea of Sardinia). As in America, to meet demand for seafood on the island, more and more fish is farm-raised. Shrimp, sea bass, mullet—much of it now comes from fields not the sea. So when you see "Mare Sardo," you know you have the flavor of the wild. And if the fisherman wants to prove it, he will open the stomach for you and say "Look. See what he ate!" He takes pride in his catch and its origin the same way a butcher in Orosei would say to my mother, "Here, I saved this from Antonia's calf." This recipe is a tribute to the fishermen of Cagliari and uses a wild fish from the Mediterranean, saragu. Buy it if you can find it—it is always "Mare Sardo."

◇   ◇   ◇

In a large saucepan, heat olive oil over medium-high heat. Add onions and garlic and cook until softened. Stir in tomato paste and the wine. Cook for 5 minutes.

Pour in vegetable stock and bring to a boil. Stir in parsley, capers, and bay leaf and let simmer for 10 minutes. Reduce heat to medium-low.

Add white bream fillets and salt to taste. Cook for 8 to 10 minutes or until fish is cooked through and sauce is thickened. Place fish on a serving plate and serve sauce over fish.

4 tablespoons extra virgin olive oil
1 white onion, chopped
2 garlic cloves, thinly sliced
1 tablespoon tomato paste
1 cup dry white wine
2 cups vegetable stock
½ bunch parsley, finely chopped
½ cup capers, drained
1 bay leaf
4 white bream fillets (or red snapper fillets)
    (6 to 8 ounces each)
1 teaspoon sea salt

THE PORT OF CAGLIARI

Cagliari is the capital of Sardinia and our largest city (around 300,000 people). As home to a vast number of archeological sites, architectural treasures, churches, and museums, not to mention our professional soccer team (Cagliari Calcio), it is the island's thriving cultural center. But Cagliari is best known as one of the most important and highly coveted ports in the Mediterranean. It was founded as a Phoenician trading colony in the seventh century BC, and since then, every invader from the Romans and Byzantines to the Germans and French has sought to control its prime location in the south of the island and the center of the sea and its access to our mountains and fertile plains. Thus, even though Cagliari has thrived as a port for nearly three thousand years, its people share the Sardinian distrust of the sea. Most of the city's development is inland, up on a hill and away from the water and its "trouble."

Sea bream with bottarga
Orata kin Buttariga

SERVES 4

Sea bream is a popular Mediterranean fish found all around Sardinia. To meet demand, it is also farmed on the island. To be sure you have wild sea bream, look at the stomach. Farm-raised fish have fatty stomachs—they live in cages. Sea bream from the wild are lean from swimming—they look like they could still jump out of the boat. Once you have your wild fish, serve them this way. My daughter Francesca, who has eaten slices of bottarga since she was three, loves this dish, which combines grated and sliced bottarga with white wine and dill to accentuate the delicate flavor of the fish.

◇　◇　◇

Preheat oven to 350°F.

Coat bottom of a baking dish with 2 tablespoons of the olive oil. Place fillets in a baking dish. Sprinkle evenly with dill, thyme, and garlic. Cover and refrigerate for at least 2 hours.

Drizzle the fillets evenly with the remaining 4 tablespoons of olive oil, then sprinkle with grated bottarga. Cook in preheated oven for 8 to 10 minutes or until fish flakes easily when prodded.

Serve drizzled with cooking liquids and topped with shavings of bottarga.

6 tablespoons extra virgin olive oil

4 sea bream fillets (6 to 8 ounces each)

¼ cup finely chopped dill

6 sprigs thyme, leaves only

2 garlic cloves, minced

¼ cup grated bottarga di muggine (see page 30)

1 ounce whole bottarga di muggine (see page 30), thinly sliced

Stuffed trout
Trota Prena
SERVES 4

I come from a land of shepherds, but seafood is my real passion. My favorite dishes are spaghetti with bottarga and Catalan-style lobster. Growing up, I secretly longed for the Festival of Santa Maria of the Sea more than any other. I savored the times my father made a big pot of mussels or when my mother bought red mullet for my birthday. Nothing makes me happier than to see islanders embracing the bounty of the sea. But demand has its repercussions and overfishing has led to depleted stocks: now conservation efforts are underway to protect the coasts and fish. When I was a boy, our rivers used to be filled with trout and eel, and my mother would make this dish, stuffing it with whatever fresh ingredients were available and the pine nuts we gathered from along the coast. Today, trout is harder to find (and is even farmed), but hopefully these recipes and memories of what used to be will preserve these flavors for generations to come.

◊　◊　◊

Preheat oven to 350°F.

Rinse the trout under running water, making sure scales are removed.

Lay out a piece of parchment paper and place two sprigs of thyme and one sprig of rosemary in the center. Place one fish skin side down on top of the herbs. Brush evenly with olive oil and sprinkle with 1 tablespoon of the grated bottarga. Repeat with the remaining fish, herbs, and bottarga.

Evenly divide arugula, basil, sun-dried tomatoes, pine nuts, anchovies, and cheese over the four fish.

Fold one side of each fish over its stuffing, making sure to hold closed with fingers to keep stuffing from spilling out. Roll parchment paper tightly over fish and wrap with aluminum foil, crimping ends to seal.

Place prepared fish in a large baking dish. Cook in preheated oven for 25 minutes or until fish flakes easily when prodded. Open and discard herbs; slice each fish diagonally into 2 or 3 pieces and place on a platter. In a small bowl, combine lemon juice and fruttato olive oil then drizzle over the fish. Finish with a sprinkling of sea salt.

4 whole trout, butterflied with skin on, cleaned and filleted

8 sprigs thyme

4 sprigs rosemary

1 to 2 tablespoons extra virgin olive oil

4 tablespoons grated bottarga di muggine (see page 30)

1½ cups coarsely chopped arugula

4 sprigs basil, leaves only, chopped

6 sun-dried tomatoes, julienned

¼ cup pine nuts, toasted

8 anchovy fillets, chopped

½ cup grated young Pecorino Sardo cheese (or other pecorino cheese)

Juice of ½ lemon

4 tablespoons fruttato extra virgin olive oil (see page 40)

Sea salt

THE SEA (NOTHING BUT TROUBLE)

My love of seafood not withstanding, Sardinian wariness of the sea marked my childhood and even pervades my town's fables. In the widely told tale of Sant'Gavino (St. Gavino), he arrives on horseback at the sea and then flies on his horse to the bridge in order to warn the townspeople of an impending invasion. Townspeople say his horse left footprints on the stone wall of the bridge and at the top of the hill nearby, where he built a church to show his love for Orosei. Today, children ride their bikes to the bridge or up the hill to the church to gaze at the giant hoof prints—just as I did years ago.

Spiny lobster salad with tomatoes and basil
Aligusta Saporita

SERVES 4

Mannoi Arre was a mason, and when he closed on a big job, he would immediately go to the market and proudly return home carrying a spiny lobster in each hand. "Here," he said to my grandmother. "Cook them!" And she or my aunt would prepare this dish while my grandfather sat and waited at the table with a glass of red wine, ready for his celebratory meal. Today, my family still celebrates everything from a birthday to a wonderful day at the beach with a meal of spiny lobster. They are seasonal and expensive but worth every penny, especially when prepared in this salad. Versions of this dish are found wherever you find the lobsters but especially on the west coast in Alghero, near Sassari, where the lobsters are the best. And of course, everyone claims to have the "original recipe." This is my favorite presentation, and though it is in no way the original, it is very tasty.

◇　◇　◇

Boil lobsters in boiling salted water for 7 minutes or until shells are bright red. Transfer immediately to a bowl of ice water to stop the cooking process and cool.

Split lobsters lengthwise in half with a sharp knife and remove corals, if present; set aside. Remove and discard vein and any other impurities. Cut each lobster into 8 to 10 pieces and place into a bowl. Add onions, tomatoes, arugula, and basil.

In a small bowl, whisk together olive oil, white wine vinegar, and lemon juice. Pour vinaigrette over lobster mixture and toss to coat well. Cover and refrigerate for at least 2 hours.

Toss salad again and add salt and pepper to taste. Mix any reserved corals with the single-orchard olive oil and drizzle over salad before serving.

2 spiny lobsters (about 1 pound each)
2 extra large green onions, white part only, sliced
6 Roma tomatoes, cored, seeded, and cut into wedges
1 bunch arugula, chopped
1 bunch basil, chopped
½ cup extra virgin olive oil
1 tablespoon white wine vinegar
Juice of 1 lemon
⅓ cup single-orchard extra virgin olive oil (see page 40)
Sea salt and freshly ground black pepper

SPINY LOBSTER

Sassari is the second largest city in Sardinia. It is home to our university and second only to Cagliari in terms of the number of cultural institutions it houses. But it is second to none in terms of lobster. The fishermen of Alghero in the Sassari region are renowned as the finest trappers of Sardinia's spiny lobster, which has a body similar to the "Maine" lobsters you find in America but does not have the two claws in front. The Sassari region was also the heart of the Catalan empire on the island, and in many towns the dialect and even the language itself are heavily influenced by Catalan.

Tuna with herbs and peppers
Filettos de Tonno
SERVES 4

Though nothing comparable to Sardinia's tuna capitals of Carloforte in the south and Olbia in the north, the gulf of Orosei is also home to tuna. The more common palamita tuna appear in our little market during the summer. They are much smaller than the prized yellowfin, with large eyes and a darker flesh. The fisherman of the town just cut them in half, not into steaks, to sell. Today, I love sushi, but growing up I did not know nor would I care what "sushi grade" meant. Nor would I eat a tuna steak rare. Like other kids, I craved this family-style dish made from the freshest summer ingredients and the tuna's flavorful and less expensive dark meat.

Coat bottom of a large sauté pan with a thin layer of olive oil. Place pan over medium-high heat until oil is smoking hot. Place tuna pieces into the pan and sear both sides about 30 seconds per side. Remove tuna pieces from heat and set aside.

In another sauté pan, heat the ¼ cup of olive oil over medium-high heat. Add garlic and heat until golden. Add anchovies to the pan and stir until dissolved. Pour in the wine and cook until alcohol evaporates. Stir in green onions, peppers, and tomatoes and toss well. Stir in lemon juice, parsley, and oregano and combine well.

Add the tuna and season to taste. Reduce heat to medium, cook for about 5 minutes or until tuna is cooked to desired doneness. Serve tuna and vegetables drizzled with the sauce.

¼ cup extra virgin olive oil, plus more for searing

2 pounds yellowfin tuna steaks, cut into 8 pieces

4 garlic cloves, thinly sliced

6 anchovies

½ cup white wine

1 bunch green onions, white part only, thinly sliced

1 cup Italian Longhorn peppers (or banana peppers), seeded, julienned

2 cups teardrop tomatoes, (or cherry tomatoes), halved

Juice of 1 lemon

½ bunch flat leaf parsley, finely chopped

3 sprigs oregano, leaves only, chopped

THE TUNA OF CARLOFORTE

The town of Carloforte on the island of San Pietro is one of the most important tuna areas in the Mediterranean, and home to one of the oldest seafaring traditions in Sardinia. That's because the fishermen of Carloforte do not share our ancient suspicion of the sea: they hail from the Ligurian colony of Tabarka, now part of Tunisia in North Africa, an area famous for its tuna fishermen. They arrived almost three centuries ago on San Pietro (the island had been deserted since Roman times), when Carlo Emanuele III offered the island to the Ligurians. Today, they remain so skilled and the tuna they catch is of such high quality that Japanese buyers come here to select yellowfin for their finest sushi houses. May and June are the peak months—when the tuna swims north past San Pietro—which is also when Carloforte holds the annual tuna festival: the Girotonno. The highlight is the magnificent *mattanza* or catching of the fish when the fishermen bring in the tuna by hand using a giant net.

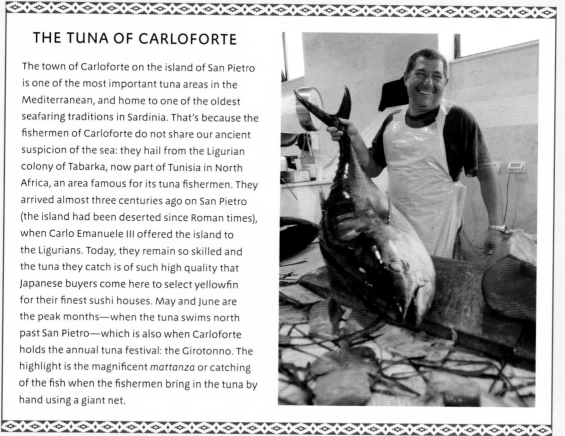

Grey mullet roasted over an open fire
Muggine Arrustu
SERVES 4

The grey mullet is Sardinia's star not because it is affordable and tasty, but because its roe produces our legendary bottarga. In Orosei, the grey mullet spawn in the Cedrino River and then head into the sea's well-oxygenated waters, where the fish develops its flavor. My father would catch it in the river when it returned and cook it right there over an open flame with just a little salt and olive oil. This recipe honors that memory, combined with another traditional way of serving grey mullet by submerging the fish in brine just after it is cooked. The brine infuses the fish with flavor and adds pleasing moistness. Serve the meal outside, eat it with your hands, and if you like, imagine you are with my father on a Sardinian beach in the early evening.

◈   ◈   ◈

Rinse the fish well under running water.

Heat the grill.

Prepare a baking dish with 4 cups of warm water. Dissolve sea salt in the water. Add garlic, parsley, bay leaves, and lemon juice; stir well and set aside.

When the grill is hot, cook fish 6 to 8 minutes or until cooked through, turning once. Immediately submerge cooked fish in the prepared water, to infuse with flavor. Bring back to the grill for 1 minute.

Serve drizzled with fruttato olive oil.

4 grey mullet, about 10 to 12 ounces each (or branzino), cleaned
1 tablespoon sea salt
6 garlic cloves, coarsely chopped
½ bunch flat leaf parsley, chopped
2 bay leaves, chopped
Juice of 1 lemon
4 tablespoons fruttato extra virgin olive oil (see page 40)

Marinated grey mullet
Muggine Marinatu
SERVES 4

There are two other traditional ways my family and the fishermen of Orosei and Cabras served our star of the sea, the grey mullet. The first is su merca: the fish is poached in salted water and then wrapped in ziba leaves to preserve it. (Ziba is a fragrant local weed from the marsh that unfortunately has no equivalent here.) The second is this one, marinating the fish in a tangy vinegar sauce that gives it an appealing brightness (a technique that also works for other fatty fish or eel). It is also an extremely versatile dish that can be eaten immediately while hot or refrigerated overnight and served cold, over a bed of hot or cold collard greens respectively.

◇ ◇ ◇

Place fillets in a baking dish and toss with 2 tablespoons of the olive oil, dill, oregano, and thinly sliced garlic. Cover and refrigerate overnight (at least 8 hours).

In a large sauté pan, heat 4 tablespoons of olive oil, add the 2 cracked garlic cloves, and cook until browned to flavor oil. Remove from heat and let cool. Return to medium heat and carefully add white wine vinegar, bay leaves, and parsley. Simmer for 10 minutes.

Preheat oven to 350°F.

Remove fish from refrigerator and drizzle with remaining 2 tablespoons of olive oil and lemon juice. Sprinkle with a pinch of sea salt and bake for 10 to 12 minutes or until fish flakes easily when prodded.

Pour sauce over the fish and serve immediately; or pour sauce over fish, let cool, and refrigerate at least 12 hours and serve cold.

4 grey mullet fillets (6 to 8 ounces each), skin on, each cut in 2 pieces
8 tablespoons extra virgin olive oil
2 tablespoons chopped dill
2 sprigs oregano, leaves only
4 garlic cloves (2 thinly sliced and 2 cracked)
¼ cup white wine vinegar
2 fresh bay leaves, chopped
½ bunch flat leaf parsley, coarsely chopped
Juice of ½ lemon
Sea salt

Whole fish in rock salt
Piske a Sale
SERVES 4

When I cut limpids and clams from the rocks, I eat the meat and drink the salt water inside the shells. The salty air and taste of the sea let me know I am home. The feeling is the same when I open the salt crust on the fish in this recipe. As the fish bakes, the rock salt forms a womb of sorts, keeping the fish moist and infusing it with the essence of the salt. (The fish itself is not salty, because the salt never penetrates the skin.) The presentation is spectacular and easy to do, especially if you know how to debone the fish. To add a little drama, mix a little egg white and water with the salt. They combine to harden the shell-like crust so that you crack it open with a hammer and a chisel. Then, drizzle the delicate fish with an extra high quality olive oil, such as a clean, spicy cold-pressed extra virgin olive oil (with just a hint of artichoke flavor).

◇   ◇   ◇

Trim the fins of the fish if they are large. Rinse well under running water; pat dry. Place rosemary and garlic cloves inside the fish.

Preheat oven to 375°F.

Place a quarter of the rock salt on the bottom of a baking dish. Place fish on top of rock salt, overlapping the cut opening to prevent salt from getting inside the fish. Cover fish with remaining rock salt. Sprinkle rock salt with water and pack closely to the fish to help create a crust.

1 whole sea bass (about 3 pounds), cleaned
1 sprig rosemary
2 garlic cloves, cracked
2 pounds rock salt
Juice of 1 lemon
4 tablespoons cold-pressed extra virgin olive oil

Place in preheated oven for **45** minutes. Test doneness by poking through salt and gently pulling out the first bone from the back of the fish. If the bone slides out easily and is warm to the touch, the fish is done.

To serve, carefully crack the salt crust without damaging the fish. Remove the salt crust to expose the entire top of the fish. Peel back skin with the edge of a large spoon. The skin should peel back easily.

Separate the two fillets from the bones. Place fillets on a warm plate or tray. In a small bowl, combine the lemon juice with the cold-pressed olive oil and drizzle over fish fillets.

THE SALT AND SARDINIA

The finest Sardinian salt comes from the marshes in Cagliari and Carloforte. But anyone who has traveled to Italy may find it surprising that you can find it in any store in Sardinia. That's because salt is controlled by the state in Italy, but not in Sardinia. As a result, while you can buy salt only from tobacconists on the mainland, you can buy it anywhere on our island, even grocery stores.

Sole with Pecorino Sardo
Palaia kin Casu de Verveke

SERVES 4

A *few of the recipes from my family and around Sardinia combine fish and cheese. To some, this is not a "natural" or familiar combination, but in Sardinia, it is a classic way to combine land and sea and can be found in traditional dishes like the fisherman's delicacy of breaded mussels from Olbia (see page 60) or eel with cheese, sage, and mint from Cagliari. In Orosei, pecorino went with sole, an easy fish to catch, clean, and skin, and which also happened to be plentiful in our gulf. This recipe comes from Zia Maria, who learned it from her mother and now makes it as a showpiece in her restaurant. To enhance the flavor of the fish, you can finish it with a sprinkling of grated bottarga (see page 30).*

◇   ◇   ◇

Remove skin from both sides of fish. Rinse well under running water; pat dry.

Preheat oven to 350°F. Grease a baking dish generously with 4 tablespoons of the butter.

In a small bowl, mix parsley and the thyme leaves.

Place fish fillets in the baking dish. Thinly slice remaining butter and divide evenly on top of fish fillets. Drizzle with olive oil. Sprinkle fish fillets with the herb mixture and freshly ground black pepper.

Bake in preheated oven for 10 minutes or until fish flakes easily when prodded. Remove from oven and divide cheese among the fillets. Place under broiler for 2 minutes for the cheese to brown. Let rest before serving.

4 whole sole (about 1 pound each), cleaned
12 tablespoons (1½ sticks) unsalted butter
4 teaspoons finely chopped flat leaf parsley
6 sprigs thyme, leaves only
¼ cup extra virgin olive oil
Freshly ground black pepper
1 cup grated Pecorino Sardo cheese (or other pecorino cheese)

My grandmother's fried salt cod
Stocafissu de Mannai

SERVES 4

My father loved it when his mother, Mannai Carta, made this winter dish. As the days grew cold, we ate pork, potatoes, eggs, and the vegetables we had preserved during the year. There was not much variety, and we often longed for something different. So when dried salt-cured cod was around, my father rejoiced. Salt cod is not native to Orosei or Sardinia, but it has been shipped to the island in barrels from Spain and around the Mediterranean for centuries. When it was available, my grandmother would take the cod and soak it in the same large pots we used to soften beans. She would then fry the softened fish and potatoes and assemble the dish exactly the same way every time: potatoes on the bottom, cod above, and the tangy sauce drizzled over the top.

◊ ◊ ◊

Soak fish fillets in fresh water overnight (at least 8 hours). Drain and pat fish dry, then cut into 8 even pieces.

Peel potatoes and cut lengthwise into 8 slices about ½ inch thick.

In a deep pan, heat vegetable oil over high heat. (Oil is ready when a small piece of bread browns in 30 seconds). Whisk egg yolks well. Dredge the fish fillets in the flour, then the beaten egg yolks, and finally in the bread crumbs, patting with hands. Fry fish fillets in batches of 2 to 3 at a time until golden, about 2 minutes, turning once. Set aside to drain on paper towels, and keep them warm. Fry potato slices until golden brown, set aside to drain on paper towels, and keep them warm.

Heat extra virgin olive oil in a sauté pan over medium heat. Add capers and tomatoes and toss well for 3 minutes. Add white wine vinegar and bring to a boil. Cook 10 minutes or until reduced and slightly thickened. Add parsley and oregano and season to taste; toss for 1 to 2 minutes for flavors to combine.

Place potato slices on the plate and top with cod fillets. Finish with the sauce. Whisk the fruttato olive oil and the lemon juice together and drizzle over fish before serving.

1½ pounds salt-cured cod fillets

3 large potatoes

4 cups vegetable oil, for frying

3 egg yolks

1 cup all-purpose flour

1 cup bread crumbs

4 tablespoons extra virgin olive oil

½ cup capers, drained

1½ cups teardrop tomatoes (or cherry tomatoes), halved

⅓ cup white wine vinegar

½ bunch flat leaf parsley, chopped

3 sprigs oregano, leaves only, chopped

Sea salt and freshly ground black pepper

¼ cup frutatto extra virgin olive oil (see page 40)

Juice of 1 lemon

Seafood stew
Zeminu
SERVES 4

Zio Pietro and I would often ride his motorcycle to the dock in the south of Orosei when the fishermen, after returning from a day at sea, stood around drinking, laughing, and telling stories. Unlike the shepherds, whose gatherings were a quiet, closed circle, fishermen were loud and boisterous—less cautious around visitors. This is how I had my first zeminu. We joined them, sharing a glass of wine and watching as they assembled this stew in a giant copper pot with each fish added in a precise order. When it was finally ready, we scooped it out with pieces of pane carasau or hard-crusted bread toasted on the grill. At home, my family made this smaller-scale version, but any similar fresh fish can be substituted. Just don't break the fish so the meat separates from the bones; instead pull them out gently. And promise me, if a fisherman invites you to enjoy the fruits of a great catch and says he is making stew, you will go.

◇　◇　◇

Slice the cuttlefish and the calamari into 1-inch strips. Cut the crab into 4 to 6 pieces, rinse well. Rinse clams and mussels thoroughly under running water to remove impurities. Clean scorpion fish and sea bass, removing guts and gills. Rinse well under running water and trim fins; slice into 4 to 6 pieces, reserving heads.

In a large deep sauté pan, heat olive oil over medium heat. Add garlic and onions and cook until onions are softened. Add cuttlefish and calamari; season with salt and cook for 2 to 3 minutes. Add the wine and simmer for 2 minutes longer. Stir in crab, clams, mussels, fish heads, and 1 cup of warm water; cook until clams begin to open, about 3 minutes.

Crush the tomatoes with a food mill or a fork and place with juices in the saucepan.

Tie the sprigs of thyme, oregano, and tarragon into a bouquet secured with kitchen twine and add to sauté pan. Stir in basil, parsley, and pepperoncino. Bring to a boil. Place scorpion fish and sea bass slices into the sauté pan, submerging under the liquid. Simmer, covered, for 10 minutes until bass pieces flake apart easily.

To serve, carefully scoop the fish from the sauté pan, place the seafood around the fish, and cover with the remaining sauce. Accompany with hard-crusted bread and finish with a drizzling of fruttato olive oil.

4 ounces cuttlefish, cleaned

4 ounces calamari, cleaned

1 blue crab

12 clams

12 mussels

1 scorpion fish (about 8 ounces)

1 sea bass (about 8 ounces)

4 tablespoons extra virgin olive oil

4 garlic cloves, cracked

1 medium onion, chopped

Sea salt

½ cup dry white wine

1 can (14.5 ounce) peeled plum tomatoes, undrained

4 sprigs thyme

2 sprigs oregano

4 sprigs tarragon

2 sprigs basil, chopped

½ bunch flat leaf parsley, chopped

1 fresh pepperoncino, chopped (or ½ teaspoon crushed red pepper)

4 pieces hard-crusted bread, toasted

Fruttato extra virgin olive oil (see page 40) for drizzling

Chicken with skinless tomatoes and pepperoncino
Puddu in Cassola

SERVES 4

Like most people in Orosei (even shepherds), my grandparents had a courtyard in the back where they kept the chickens. They always roamed free and laid their eggs in the barn where my brother Francesco and I would hunt for them in the hay. We mostly raised chickens for their eggs, which my grandfather ate right out of the shell. But sometimes—when we had too many chickens or maybe one pulled up lame or just stopped producing—we had the chicken, too. This uncomplicated stew was one of my mother's favorites to make during the week. As stews go, it is quick to make, a little spicy, and easy to prepare. Although she would use the whole chicken when we were growing up, today she gets her chickens from the market and uses the breasts for this dish, which is how I made it here.

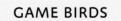

In a large nonstick skillet, heat 3 tablespoons of the olive oil over medium-high heat. Add onion and garlic cloves and cook until softened. Add chicken and thyme, tossing chicken until browned evenly.

Add chicken stock, tomatoes, pepperoncino, parsley, salt, and basil. Reduce heat to medium-low and cook, covered, for 30 minutes. Uncover and cook an additional 30 minutes. Stir frequently to prevent sticking.

Remove sprigs of thyme and garlic before serving. Finish with a drizzling of the remaining 1 tablespoon olive oil.

4 tablespoons extra virgin olive oil

1 extra large green onion, chopped

5 garlic cloves

1½ pounds boneless chicken breasts, cut into 2- to 3-inch pieces

3 sprigs thyme

1 cup chicken stock

½ pound Roma tomatoes, peeled, seeded, drained, and cut into ½-inch strips

1 fresh pepperoncino, halved (or ½ to 1 teaspoon crushed red pepper)

1 tablespoon finely chopped flat leaf parsley

Sea salt

2 sprigs basil, chopped

GAME BIRDS

My family raised chickens and hens—by large the most common poultry in Sardinia—but throughout the island and even in Orosei, game birds are also very popular. We were not hunters, but the ducks, quail, doves, and wild pigeons that thrived along the river attracted those who were. The pigeons are especially famous, and although we did not eat them very much growing up (which is why I do not include any recipes for game birds), you'll find them prepared all over the island in stews like those in this book or simply grilled on an open fire with olive oil and salt. The only exception in my family was when we trapped song thrushes in the winter time, which we would grill or my mother would bake instead of chicken in a stew.

Hen for a complete meal
Puddu a Brou
SERVES 4

Bring your family to the table the way my grandmother would on Sunday with this elaborate chicken dish, a version of what the Italians call "bollito," or a complete boiled meal. She made the whole thing in the backyard while we were at church, boiling the water, cleaning the chicken, and setting the table. The chicken is boiled first to make a broth for the soup, then the big pieces and vegetables are set aside for the main course, while the rest of the carcass is picked clean to add to the salad. Coming back home, dressed in our church best, the soup with its fregula and pecorino, chicken pieces dressed with vegetables, and salad with bits of the picked chicken and drizzled with good olive oil seemed even more beautiful and impressive–not to mention tasty–to all of us.

◊　　◊　　◊

Cut chicken into 6 to 8 pieces. Place onion, celery, carrot in a large stock pot. Add chicken pieces. Fill stock pot three-quarters full with water (about 12 cups); add 1 tablespoon salt. Bring to boil, skim fat from the top. Add parsley, bay leaf, and sun-dried tomatoes. Reduce heat to low, cover, and cook for 2 hours.

Strain broth through a sieve and reserve. Set breasts, legs, thighs and vegetables aside and keep them warm. Sort through the remaining chicken, reserving the meat and discarding bones and fat.

To prepare the soup, bring 8 cups of the broth to a boil. Add saffron and fregula and boil for 10 to 12 minutes. Stir in the pecorino cheese. (The remaining stock can be kept refrigerated for 3 to 4 days or frozen.)

To prepare the salad, in a bowl toss romaine lettuce, celery, tomatoes, and reserved bits of chicken meat with extra virgin olive oil. Sprinkle with sea salt.

Arrange the cooked vegetables on a platter and top with the breasts, legs and thighs, then finish with a drizzling of olive oil and a sprinkling of sea salt.

1 hen (3 to 4 pounds), preferably free-range organic

1 medium onion, halved

3 stalks celery, cut in 2 to 3 pieces

3 carrots, cut in 2 to 3 pieces

Sea salt

4 sprigs flat leaf parsley

1 bay leaf

5 sun-dried tomatoes

½ teaspoon saffron

½ pound fregula (see page 119)

½ cup grated Pecorino Sardo cheese (or other pecorino cheese)

1 head romaine lettuce, torn

1 celery heart, roughly chopped

8 teardrop tomatoes (or cherry tomatoes), halved

2 to 3 tablespoons extra virgin olive oil

CHICKEN FOR DINNER

To welcome our guests, we typically serve the best of what our shepherds and the sea has to offer—pecorino, lamb, malloreddus with bottarga—instead of the chickens from our own yards. In my home and throughout Sardinia, chicken dishes were the centerpiece of many special family meals and evoke fond memories, but still they are rarely dressed for more than family. Even today, if a friend of my father's unexpectedly stays for lunch, my mother would sooner bring out suckling pig before making chicken. This is also why you rarely see an article on Sardinia featuring chicken recipes; instead, the fare typically depicted is pasta, lamb, pork, or seafood.

Hen cooked with Vernaccia
Puddu kin Vernaccia de Oristano
SERVES 4

My mother always made this stew using the whole hen. Perhaps she used more onions and fewer chives than I prefer, but she always added that wonderful old dry bottle of Vernaccia she had in the back of the pantry to give the dish its spiciness and distinctive aroma. My mother usually made this dish for dinner, but my favorite memory of this meal is when she would wrap the pot with a kitchen towel and we'd take it to the beach for a picnic lunch.

◇　◇　◇

Cut the hen into 6 to 8 pieces. In a terra-cotta pot or Dutch oven, heat olive oil over medium-high heat. Add onions and cook until brown. Add the hen and brown evenly, sprinkling with one teaspoon of sea salt.

Reduce heat to low. Add wine, then add the vegetable stock, making sure the meat is covered. Season with remaining teaspoon of salt. Cover and cook for 2 hours, occasionally stirring. Stir in parsley and chives; cook for 5 minutes longer. Turn off heat, cover, and let sit 15 minutes before serving.

Serve drizzled with the cooking liquids.

1 hen (3 to 4 pounds), preferably free-range organic
¼ cup extra virgin olive oil
1 onion, chopped
2 teaspoons sea salt
1½ cups Vernaccia Secca wine (or Malvasia wine)
1 cup vegetable stock
1 bunch flat leaf parsley, finely chopped
1 bunch chives, chopped

THE GRAPE HARVEST & WINEMAKING

My family always had (and still does) a bottle of intense Malvasia from Bosa or warm amber Vernaccia from Oristano in addition to our own homemade wine for drinking, cooking, and welcoming guests to the table. My family's grapes were Cannonau, a strong red wine grape, and I am happy to serve our wine in my restaurants: Every bottle is flavored by my fond memories of the grape harvest and winemaking. The harvest day started when the whole family headed to our vineyard. It was like a final holiday before school started—the last bit of summer before the days got colder and shorter. We carried a picnic lunch of sausage and cheese and some macarrones de busa—and, to celebrate a great harvest, some suckling pig. We worked the whole day picking fruit, putting it in baskets, emptying the baskets into the ox cart, and then going back for more. Back in town, we placed the grapes in buckets and my brother Francesco and I stomped them into juice, which might have been more fun if not for the bees swarming around us. When we finished stomping, we still weren't done. We washed off our legs and carried the buckets of juice to the wine barrels in the cantina, the bees chasing us every step of the way. (For more on the typical varietals of Sardinia, see page 130.)

Eggs with onions and tomatoes
Ovos kin Achipudda

SERVES 4

Both egg recipes in this book are centuries-old peasant dishes. This one, which calls for cooking eggs in tomato sauce, is the other recipe my father loves to make (his specialty is cozzas a sa moda de Babbu, page 62). When you don't have lunch ready, eggs are the quickest way to make a meal. When I first saw him make it, he used the fruity spring onions from our garden. He trimmed the onions roughly with his pocketknife, which gave them a rustic look. Then he grabbed my mother's tomato sauce from the pantry to cook the eggs. He ate the finished dish off the plate using pane carasau as a scoop just as the peasants would. I like to eat it that way, too, but also add a little grated bottarga at the end to make it a little more special.

◇ ◇ ◇

In a large saucepan, heat 2 tablespoons of the olive oil over medium heat. Add garlic and onions and cook until onion is golden. In a bowl, crush canned tomatoes with a food mill or a fork, discarding any unripened pieces. Add tomatoes and bay leaf; simmer for 15 minutes.

Remove garlic and stir in basil; season with salt and pepper to taste. Crack each egg on top of the tomato sauce, leaving space in between. Cover and cook until eggs are cooked to desired doneness.

Serve eggs over pieces of pane carasau and with any remaining sauce. Sprinkle eggs with the grated bottarga and a drizzling of remaining 2 tablespoons olive oil.

4 tablespoons extra virgin olive oil

2 garlic cloves, cracked

2 extra large green onions, thinly sliced

2 cans (14.5 ounces each) peeled plum tomatoes, undrained

1 bay leaf

2 sprigs basil, chopped

Sea salt and freshly ground black pepper

4 eggs

4 sheets pane carasau (see page 22), broken in pieces

2 tablespoons grated bottarga di muggine (see page 30)

Pane carasau with tomato sauce, pecorino, and poached eggs
Pane Frattau

SERVES 4

My American friends call this a perfect brunch recipe. Sardinians don't eat brunch, but you will find a version of this traditional peasant dish everywhere on the island. It combines four things almost every home has: some pane carasau, tomatoes, pecorino, and eggs. Some versions may have different names and personal twists from the cook or chef, but the foundation of these four ingredients is always the same. This version with a poached egg on top is my son Valerio's all-time favorite. It also displays the versatility of pane carasau; in this case, softened by dipping in broth, it has a noodlelike consistency. Remember: pane frattau must be served hot, so make sure you boil the water for poaching the eggs while you are assembling the rest of the dish.

◊   ◊   ◊

Heat tomato sauce to boil. In a separate saucepan, bring broth to a slow boil.

In another large saucepan, bring about 5 cups of water to a simmer. Warm the serving plates.

Break each pane carasau sheet into 5 pieces.

To build each pane frattau, dip two pieces of the pane carasau in the meat broth. Place bread on a warmed serving plate. Layer tomato sauce on the bread and top with some pecorino cheese. Dip two more of the pieces in the broth; layer on the plate with the tomato sauce and cheese. Repeat with final piece of bread, sauce, and cheese.

Build the remaining plates in the same process.

Poach the eggs individually in the simmering water until they reach desired stage of doneness. Remove each with a slotted spoon and place one egg on each plate of bread layers. Sprinkle with chopped basil. Drizzle with olive oil and sprinkle egg yolk with sea salt.

2 cups tomato sauce (see recipe, page 92)
2 cups lamb broth (see recipe, page 71) (or beef or vegetable stock)
4 round sheets pane carasau (see page 22)
1 cup finely grated Pecorino Sardo cheese (or other pecorino cheese)
4 eggs
8 sprigs basil, finely chopped (about ⅓ cup)
4 tablespoons extra virgin olive oil
Sea salt

Fava beans with peppermint
Ava Frisca kin Menta

SERVES 4

I remember my grandmother and my mother making this recipe as soon as the first juicy, sweet fava beans arrived in the spring. Beans and mint are a natural and ancient combination in Sardinia. The spice of the mint fascinates me and makes this simple recipe special. We use mint to flavor familiar dishes like lamb, but we also use it in our honey, with vegetables like fennel, and in soups like suppa de su pastore (see page 40). In this recipe, it is essential that you not overcook the beans, otherwise you will lose it all—the flavor and the texture of the dish.

◇   ◇   ◇

In a large skillet, heat olive oil over medium-high heat. Add onion and cook until softened, about 1 minute. Add the fava beans and ¾ cup water to cover. Sprinkle with sea salt and parsley. Stir to combine.

Reduce heat to medium-low and simmer for 20 minutes or until all water is absorbed. Add peppermint and stir for 2 minutes to incorporate.

Serve over pane carasau and finish with grated ricotta salata.

- 2 tablespoons extra virgin olive oil
- 1 extra large green onion, white part only, minced
- 1 pound fresh fava beans, shelled
- ¼ teaspoon sea salt
- 1 tablespoon chopped flat leaf parsley
- 2 sprigs peppermint, torn
- 2 sheets pane carasau (see page 22), broken into 4 pieces each
- 2 ounces ricotta salata cheese, grated

CORK PLATES

When I visited my sister Angela in Nuoro early one spring, I immediately thought of making fresh fava beans in mint and a traditional shepherd dish called *fava con lardo*—a stew of the fatty pig shoulder and neck (skin on), boiled potatoes, kale, and dried fava beans. Keeping with tradition, Angela served it on an *avaione* or cork plate that shepherds use and then wipe off and hang to dry until the next meal. The cork looks porous, but it is not; even with a brothy dish like fava con lardo, the plate never absorbs the liquid, leaving it ready to be sopped up by the pane carasau.

Greens with pancetta
Irvuzu

SERVES 4

The greens in this recipe—fennel, chicory, dill, rapini, escarole, and wild asparagus—are my "soul" food. It warms my heart just thinking of the moments my father and I would hunt for them on the hillsides by the Cedrino River, looking for the spaces and shaded corners where no one had been or the sheep had not gotten to. And just as these greens combine in nature to "flavor" the land, they are wonderful together on the plate steamed and sautéed, enhanced with just a little pancetta and garlic. Alone or with some roasted sausage they are, as my wife has taught me to say, "to die for."

◇　◇　◇

Wash greens thoroughly and roughly chop into large pieces.

Boil greens in lightly salted water for 5 minutes. Drain well.

In a deep sauté pan, heat olive oil over medium heat. Add pancetta and cook until the fat has rendered. Add garlic and cook until golden. Stir in greens and sauté for 3 minutes. Season with salt to taste; finish with a drizzling of fruttato olive oil.

2 pounds mixed greens (preferably fennel, chicory, dill, rapini, escarole, and thin asparagus)

2 tablespoons extra virgin olive oil

¼ pound pancetta, diced

5 garlic cloves, halved

Sea salt

1 to 2 tablespoons fruttato extra virgin olive oil (see page 40)

Asparagus fritters
Zippulas de Isparau
SERVES 4

When wild asparagus appear in February and March, finding the food is second to the fun of the hunt—a tradition in my family. But we never knew what we were going to get. In the years when the asparagus was plentiful, we combed the hills of Orosei around the muri a secco (low stone walls) that divided the properties every chance we got. If we spotted a fresh cut, we knew someone was ahead of us, so we turned and went in another direction. On the days when the gathering was good, we would come home with so many asparagus that my mother had to find many different ways to prepare them. These light and fluffy fritters were one of my favorites. She made them all the time for breakfast, lunch, a snack, or dinner.

◇　◇　◇

Trim asparagus and rinse well. Blanch for 2 minutes in salted boiling water, then transfer immediately to a bowl filled with ice water to stop the cooking process. Cut spears into 3- to 4-inch pieces and pat dry.

In a large bowl, stir a pinch of salt into the flour. Add eggs and milk and stir until incorporated. Add asparagus and toss to coat evenly.

In a large pan, heat vegetable oil over high heat (oil is ready when a small piece of bread browns in 30 seconds). Drop battered asparagus by the spoonful into the vegetable oil and cook until golden brown, turning once. Set on paper towels to drain and cool.

> 1½ pounds asparagus (pencil thin)
> Sea salt
> 2 cups semolina flour
> 3 eggs
> 1 cup milk
> Vegetable oil for frying

KNIVES

When I go hunting asparagus or any wild greens in Sardinia, I never forget my knife—no Sardinian ever would. We treat knives like a part of our hands. The traditional Sardinian knife is called *sa leppa*—a hinged knife with handles of black or brown ram horn and a blade of sharp steel ready to cut chicory or fennel or anything else we might encounter on a hike. Thus, we take great pride in the ancient art of forging knives, and artisans like the legendary Fogarizzu who make them often sign the blades and sell them in person at festivals. It is considered a great honor to buy or receive one of these knives. (Often you have to know someone, who knows someone, to find them.) And if you do receive one as a gift, the custom is to give that person a coin, both as a token of gratitude and for good luck—after all, you just handed someone a knife!

Summer zucchini
Curcurikedda a Cassola
SERVES 4

"Conca chi non allegat curcurica li torran," my mother says: "If you don't speak up, you get zucchini." Well, that's the literal translation. What it really means is, if you do not say anything you're going to get what you get. "How am I going to know what you want if you do not say anything?" she would say. Thus in my home, just like in school, zucchini was a metaphor for missing out. But if you ever have to "get zucchini," I hope you turn it into something at least as delicious as this recipe of my mother's, which is best made when zucchini is in full season.

◇ ◇ ◇

In a large saucepan, heat olive oil over medium heat. Add onion and cook until translucent. Add tomatoes and cook for 3 minutes. Add the wine and simmer for 2 minutes longer.

Stir in basil and bay leaves. Add zucchini and 1½ cups of water. Season with salt to taste; cover and cook 30 minutes.

Let sit 15 minutes before serving, for flavors to come together.

4 tablespoons extra virgin olive oil
1 extra large green onion, chopped
1 cup Roma tomatoes, peeled, seeded, and
  chopped
¼ cup dry white wine
2 sprigs basil, chopped
2 bay leaves
2 pounds zucchini, chopped
Sea salt

Steamed Swiss chard
Aveta kin Ozu Novu

SERVES 4

Many of the greens I grew up with are plentiful in America, and I am always surprised at how few people make them. Take Swiss chard, for example. My father has always had a piece of his garden dedicated to it so we would have it on hand as a filling for gulurjones (ravioli) or for this simple light dish made with just salt, olive oil, and some lemon juice. I don't think there has been a time in my life when I have not seen this dish in my parents' house. My mother often makes this for her dinner, or she and my father will share it for lunch. It is good served hot, warm, or cold, paired with a light fish or meat dish.

◈   ◈   ◈

Submerge Swiss chard in water and swirl to release any sandy particles. Trim away any large stems. Cut into 4- to 5-inch pieces (or small enough to fit into steamer). Place into steamer and cook for 30 minutes.

In a small bowl, whisk olive oil with lemon juice. Drizzle over steamed Swiss chard and sprinkle with a pinch of sea salt before serving.

2 pounds Swiss chard
⅓ cup extra virgin olive oil
Juice of ½ lemon
Sea salt

Eggplant with tomato and herbs
Perdinzanu Pizzarellu

SERVES 4

We ate a lot of eggplant growing up: cooked in a pot like a stew, fried with some cheese, layered like lasagna. This recipe is one of my favorites. It is like a vegetarian version of perdinzanu prenu (see page 74), and while it does not cure my homesickness the way that dish does, the smell of it cooking does remind me of my house and the food my mother loves to cook. We ate it as a side dish for fish like orata or even as an appetizer or main plate. The preparation could not be easier: throw together the raw ingredients (called "a crudo"), put them in the oven, and walk away for 45 minutes. Serve with the juices from the pan poured over the top.

Cut stem from eggplant and split in half lengthwise. Place skin side down and score the flesh, being careful not to pierce the skin. Sprinkle generously with sea salt and let sit for 2 hours for juices to purge. Rinse well and pat dry.

Preheat oven to 350°F.

Place eggplants on a baking sheet skin side down. In a large bowl, mix garlic, all herbs, tomatoes, capers, and pepperoncini and top each eggplant evenly with the mixture. Drizzle with the olive oil and sprinkle with sea salt to taste. Cook for 45 minutes in preheated oven.

Let rest a few minutes before serving for flavors to come together. This dish is excellent served either hot or cold.

2 pounds eggplant

Sea salt

6 garlic cloves, finely chopped

½ bunch flat leaf parsley, chopped

4 sprigs basil, leaves only, chopped

4 sprigs oregano, leaves only, chopped

2 cups Roma tomatoes, peeled, seeded, and chopped

¼ cup capers, drained

2 fresh pepperoncini (or ½ to 1 teaspoon of crushed red pepper)

¼ cup extra virgin olive oil

AN EGGPLANT THERMOMETER

In the afternoon during the daylong baking of pane carasau (see page 22), I remember seeing a white bowl full of eggplants come out of the house and head to the oven. There it would sit at the feet of the women of my town ready for duty—as a thermometer. You see, in those days, we had no thermostat or oven thermometer. So, in order to gauge the oven's temperature—to determine when it had cooled to the right level that would allow for proper toasting of the pane carasau—they slipped an eggplant inside. If the eggplant became charred quickly, the

women knew the oven was still too hot. But if it cooked evenly until it was uniformly soft, they knew the oven was just right. When they finished the baking, we made an eggplant mousse, which we ate that evening and for days after the baking was done. Today, I preserve this memory in my restaurants with a pizza topped with the same mousse.

Cauliflower with olives
Caule Assofocatu

SERVES 4

My elementary school was only two blocks from my house, and the short walk home was always fun, a release from a long day of sitting and learning. As I turned the corner at my house, the warm distinctive smell of cauliflower often met me. This traditional peasant recipe makes an easy side dish in late fall and early winter, when olives and cauliflower are abundant. Or eat it as a meal as my parents would, using pane carasau or crusty bread as a scoop. In Sardinia, my family used the Bosana olives from our orchards. In America, I use Kalamata olives for their strong flavor or fresh green California olives. The recipe should yield a cooked cauliflower that has absorbed all the liquid. However, since cauliflower can vary in moisture content, you may need to add additional hot water.

◊   ◊   ◊

Trim hard outer leaves and stem from cauliflower. Cut into florets and rinse well under running water.

Place cauliflower in a large saucepan and add garlic. Drizzle with olive oil and parsley. Add salt and 1½ cups water. Cover and place over medium heat; cook for 20 minutes.

Stir in olives and cook 10 minutes longer for flavors to combine.

2 pounds cauliflower

2 garlic cloves, cracked

⅓ cup extra virgin olive oil

½ bunch parsley, finely chopped

1 teaspoon sea salt

1 cup fresh Bosana olives (or other fresh olive)

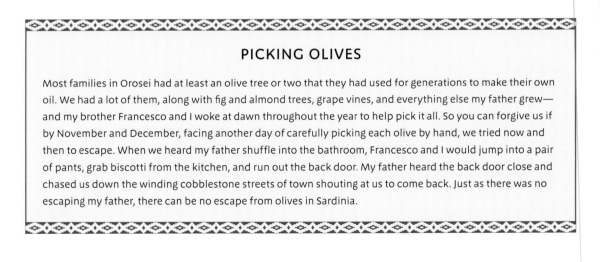

PICKING OLIVES

Most families in Orosei had at least an olive tree or two that they had used for generations to make their own oil. We had a lot of them, along with fig and almond trees, grape vines, and everything else my father grew— and my brother Francesco and I woke at dawn throughout the year to help pick it all. So you can forgive us if by November and December, facing another day of carefully picking each olive by hand, we tried now and then to escape. When we heard my father shuffle into the bathroom, Francesco and I would jump into a pair of pants, grab biscotti from the kitchen, and run out the back door. My father heard the back door close and chased us down the winding cobblestone streets of town shouting at us to come back. Just as there was no escaping my father, there can be no escape from olives in Sardinia.

Desserts
Durkes

◈

Non bat isposu senza marigosu.

"There is no wedding without a cake."

In my home, dessert was usually a little filu'e ferru or wine for
the men, a piece of candy from the pantry for the children, and
a plate of my father's dried figs or fresh fruit for all: watermelon
in summertime, oranges in winter, and maybe in late winter a
treat of winter melon or grapes we had preserved by hanging
them from the ceiling in the cucina rustica. There was always
something sweet around, but any pastries (and even that candy
for the children) tended to be left over from special occasions–
birthdays, weddings, baptisms, and especially festivals and
Carnevale. And each one was made from traditional recipes
featuring only local ingredients and passed down for generations.
The women worked for days to create them, not because the
pastries were hard to make (though the intricate shapes of some
of the special pastries are astounding), but because so many were
needed. The recipes included in this chapter are authentic, but the
portions are also a tenth, even a fiftieth, of what we made when
celebrating with family, friends, and the entire town.

Fried puffed pastry filled with sweet cheese
Seadas e Mele Rankidu

MAKES ABOUT 4 PASTRIES

Seadas are the closest we have to a national dessert in Sardinia. They have been made on the island for centuries—definitely since the Spanish occupation and possibly in the Nuraghic era. Seadas come in many versions: some are sweeter than others; some add lemon peel or herbs like mint or parsley; and some use sugar rather than bitter honey to finish them (sugar is not refined on Sardinia and is a modern substitution in our desserts). Every version, however, looks basically the same: a lightly fried disk of puffed pastry filled with a young, mild cheese. Seadas are also surprisingly light—even after sitting for a hearty three-hour Sardinian meal, I always have room for them. When I was growing up, my family made them in the spring, when the cheese was at its best. My mother never felt they were worth eating unless the fresh cheese stretched like a string when you lifted a piece to your mouth (like biting a slice of pizza). Today, another modern convenience allows us to have seadas any time we want—you can buy them frozen in markets all over the island.

◇　◇　◇

On a clean workspace, mound the flour with a well in the center. Sprinkle the salt evenly over the flour. Add the egg and ³/₄ cup warm water into the well and gradually mix into the flour with your hands. When mixture begins to come together, add the lard and olive oil and knead to fully incorporate. Cover the dough with a cloth and let rest at room temperature for 30 minutes.

In a mixing bowl, combine the cheese, zest, and mint.

On a lightly floured workspace, roll the dough out to a width of about 7 to 8 inches and with a ¹/₈-inch thickness. Using a sharp paring knife, cut into rounds, each about 6 inches in diameter. Reroll the scraps and cut again as necessary to yield a total of eight rounds. Divide the cheese mixture evenly among four of the rounds, lightly mounding it onto the center of each round. Top with the remaining dough rounds and lightly press edges together, crimping edges with a fork to seal. Lightly dust with flour to prevent sticking and set aside, covered with a cloth to prevent drying.

In a saucepan over low heat, warm the bitter honey.

In a deep heavy saucepan, add enough oil to reach a depth of about 2 inches. Place over high heat (oil is ready when a small piece of bread browns in 30 seconds). Fry seadas in two batches, turning once, until golden brown, about 5 minutes total for each pair. Remove with slotted spoon and drain on paper towels. Serve topped with warmed bitter honey.

3¾ cups all-purpose flour
Pinch of salt
1 egg
1 cup lard (or vegetable shortening)
1 tablespoon extra virgin olive oil
1 pound fresh Sardinian cheese (or mozzarella), shredded
Zest of 2 lemons, finely grated
4 sprigs mint, chopped
½ cup bitter honey (see page 229)
Vegetable oil for frying

MIELE AMARO (BITTER HONEY)

Sardinian miele amaro (bitter honey) has a distinctive aroma and complex flavor—a deep yet fleeting sweetness, followed by an appealingly bitter aftertaste. We call it "liquid gold" for its deep amber color, value to our cuisine, and medicinal qualities (we still use it as a remedy for sore throats). In Sardinia, every home has a jar from a friend or local producer in the pantry. Before refined sugar was on the island, we used honey to sweeten everything. Today, our bitter honey is most traditionally used to finish seadas and as an ingredient in other desserts, but I like it in salads and main dishes as well.

Bitter honey is made from the flowers of the corbezzolo, or strawberry trees, which grow wild along Sardinia's coast and mountain valleys. As children, we used to grab the white bell-shaped flowers from the trees and suck out the uniquely flavored pollen. Of course, we had to dodge the bees to do it. The harvest usually happens in October, when the fall rains stop but summer temperatures and long days linger. The beekeepers move the bees to the trees, and on sunny days the bees seem to be attacking the flowers. The bees need to be aggressive: they have to work hard and fast to create our gold. To make bitter honey, it takes more than 7,000 trips from hive to flower—twice as many as for regular honey—and the flower opens for pollination for only two weeks.

Fruit and ice cream with mirto
Frutta Miskia

SERVES 4

The simplest dessert we make is the perfect way to savor one of the most important flavors of the Sardinian culinary landscape: take a scoop of vanilla ice cream, top it with fresh fruit, and drizzle it with mirto—the quintessential Sardinian after-dinner drink. Virtually unknown in the United States, mirto is sacred to us. It is made by macerating the berry of our signature plant—mirto (myrtle)—in sugar, water, and alcohol for around six weeks. (The berries ripen from November through January and are picked by hand before processing.) The resulting purple drink is strong and thick, fragrant and somewhat sweet. It is served cold, over ice, to cleanse your palate after a meal or to refresh you on a hot day while sitting in an outdoor café. My father makes his, of course, and it is still my favorite. But my father's mirto may be a little hard to come by for you. As a substitute, look for a bottle from Lucrezio R., a Berchidda distillery owned by my friends the Raus, which is dedicated to preserving the traditional methods of production.

◇ ◇ ◇

In a large bowl, combine the fruit with the citrus juices, sugar, and mint and toss to coat evenly. Place in the refrigerator for at least 2 hours for flavors to combine.

Divide the cold fruit evenly among four dishes. Top each dish with a scoop of ice cream and drizzle with the mirto liqueur before serving.

4 cups assorted seasonal fruit (any mix of strawberries, blueberries, or raspberries, and diced pears, figs, or prickly pear)
Juice of 1 orange
Juice of 1 lemon
1 tablespoon sugar
4 to 5 sprigs fresh mint, finely chopped
1 pint of vanilla or fruit ice cream
4 tablespoons mirto liqueur

MIRTO

An evergreen common throughout the Mediterranean, myrtle covers Sardinia—near the sea and on the mountain slopes, along the hills and riverbanks—and Sardinians use myrtle to flavor everything. We use its leaves to flavor roast meat, particularly suckling pig (see pages 166 and 168); we use its tannic, seed-filled berries, which have a flavor similar to juniper, to make our liqueur and preserves; and we use its aromatic wood for spits and to fill our fireplaces. In addition, its oil has medicinal qualities, and its white flowers flavor the spring air. To me, myrtle means home. Wandering the island, I cannot help stopping at the bushes, grabbing the leaves in my hand, crunching them up, and inhaling. It's an intoxicating aroma no Sardinian ever tires of—an irresistibly sweet perfume, distinctive and engaging, warm and comforting. So much so, I had to plant my own myrtle here, to flavor not only our food but my memories of home. The branches and leaves can usually be found at

wholesale florists and some nurseries. (Ask for Mediterranean myrtle, *Myrtus communis*, not the more common crape myrtle found in the United States.)

CARRASECARE

Carrasecare, better known as Carnival season or Carnevale, runs from the Festival of St. Anthony (the evening of January 16) through Mardi Gras, and in the eight days leading up to Fat Tuesday, the island fills with celebrations. Even the smallest mountain villages have important traditions (see Seneghe on page 171), while some of the largest and most famous festivals—Sos Mamuthones in Mamoiada, Sos Merdules in Ottana, Sa Sartiglia in Oristano—involve hundreds, even thousands of participants and spectators, and date back to medieval times.

During Carnevale in Orosei, the children wear costumes with masks and parents take them around town to visit friends and family. Every house offers up pastries and candies, and the hosts try to guess whose face each mask hides. When I was a boy, I always knew the "special" houses to call on first—which ones had the best sweets to share with the children and a glass of the just-ready new wine to offer the adults. For me, Carnevale was something to look forward to between Christmas and Easter, especially for the food and the three signature desserts in my family: orillettas, vuvusones, and gulurjones durkes. Of course, with Zia Mary and Zia Zizzi leading our family's dessert creation, our house was among the most popular. My father would pour his wine and trays of our desserts disappeared in minutes. Sticky with honey, they were always lick-your-fingers-good—and still are.

Fried pastry braids
Orillettas

MAKES 8 TO 10 PASTRIES

Fried and drizzled with honey, orillettas are like eating a sticky, very flaky piecrust. My sister Angela now makes these for our family during Carnevale, and her only modern concession is that she uses a pasta machine to flatten the dough into long pieces. She then cuts the decorative edges for her beautiful braids using sa rudillia—an ancient handmade tool now made by only a few artisans in Sardinia. Though it resembles a small pizza cutter, sa rudillia has a fluted decorative blade that also crimps as it cuts (for filled pastries and pastas). Once you've mastered this basic recipe, you can experiment, using a crimping pastry wheel, with creating more elaborate shapes such as the floral crown shown in the picture below at right.

◇ ◇ ◇

On a clean workspace, mound the flour and stir in sugar. Make a well in the center. Gently whisk the egg yolks in a small bowl, pour into the well and gradually mix into the flour with your hands. When the mixture begins to come together, add the olive oil and knead to fully incorporate.

> 3¼ cups all-purpose flour
> ¾ cup sugar
> 3 egg yolks
> ½ cup extra virgin olive oil
> Vegetable oil for frying
> Powdered sugar for dusting or honey for
>   drizzling

Working with small sections of dough and keeping extra dough covered, roll the dough into short ropes, each about 6 inches long and about ¼ to ½ inch in diameter–you should have between 24 and 30. Braid three pieces together and press ends to secure. Lightly dust with flour and set aside. Repeat with the remaining pieces of dough.

In a deep heavy saucepan, add enough oil to reach a depth of about 2 inches. Place over high heat (oil is ready when a small piece of bread browns in 30 seconds). Fry the orillettas in batches of three, turning once until pastry begins to float and turn golden. Set on paper towels to drain and serve dusted with sugar or drizzled with honey.

Fluffy fried pastry spirals
Vuvusones

MAKES ABOUT 4 PASTRIES

Vuvusones are like Sardinian funnel cakes, and they are a specialty of Zia Mary's. She would spend hours kneading the dough then piping it into the hot oil to create a spiral. Like so many of my aunts' desserts, I could never wait for them to be served. In this case, I would sneak into the kitchen as they cooled and cut a little piece for myself.

◈ ◈ ◈

On a clean workspace, mound the flour with a well in the center. Dissolve the yeast in ¹/₂ cup warm water. Add the yeast, eggs, and milk into the well and gradually mix into the flour with your hands. When the mixture begins to come together, add the filu'e ferru and sambuca and knead to fully incorporate. Place the dough in a large bowl and cover with a clean linen towel. Let the dough rest and rise until doubled in size.

In a deep heavy saucepan, add enough oil to reach a depth of about 3 inches. Place over high heat (oil is ready when a small piece of bread browns in 30 seconds).

Put all of dough into a large pastry bag fitted with a plain ¹/₂-inch-wide tip. Very carefully, pipe a rope of dough into the oil, starting from the center of the oil and spiraling outwards in a snail-like formation, but leaving a small space between the rings so the dough does not stick to itself and cooks evenly. Keep spiraling until the circle is about 5 inches in diameter.

Fry, turning once, until the pastry begins to float and turns golden, 3 to 4 minutes. Remove the spiral with a slotted spoon. Set on paper towels to drain. Repeat process three more times so you end up with four fried spirals of dough. Serve hot, dusted with sugar.

3¾ cups all-purpose flour

2 teaspoons active dry yeast

3 eggs

¼ cup milk, room temperature

1 tablespoon filu'e ferru (see page 170) (or grappa or brandy)

1 tablespoon sambuca liqueur

Vegetable oil for frying

Granulated sugar for dusting

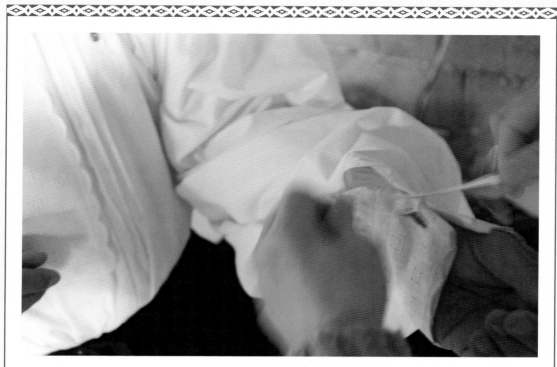

DRESSING UP THE ISLAND

From intricately woven rugs to finely embroidered scarves, Sardinians are masterful manufacturers of textiles and clothing (not to mention keepers of many arts and crafts traditions, from musical instruments to jewelry). The costumes of Sardinia that you see during Carnevale festivals not only put our ancient sewing skills on full display but also recall a time when "costumes" were more than just outfits for a parade.

When I was growing up, my father and I did not wear the "costume" of Orosei: white shirt and pants covered below the calf with black stockings and a skirt above the knee with a red and black vest and a black hat on top. But my father told me that when he was young, people wore this costume on an everyday basis. In other words, your costume was your wardrobe and every town had different combinations of designs, materials, and colors—lighter colors and fabrics toward the coast, darker and heavier ones in the mountains. (Orgosolo's are particularly ornate.) Shepherds wore suits of velvet, which were comfortable, warm, and dark and withstood the elements. At weddings and festivals, the elaborate dress costumes came out, each adorned with jewelry made from coral and other gems (called the *filogran*—Sardinians literally wore their wealth on their sleeves).

Today, those shepherd suits and vests are a fashion statement—made by only a few artisans, such as Modolo in Orani where I get my suits and the vests for my restaurants' uniforms. And a group of young people has formed the Ballos in Costume to preserve some of the traditions by hosting dances in costume in town squares around the island.

Sweet ravioli with bitter honey
Gulurjones Durkes

MAKES 12 TO 16 PASTRIES

These dense, flaky, and slightly sweet ravioli of Zia Mary's are so good, I have never known someone who can eat just ten. Filled with creamy, sweetened ricotta and drizzled with bitter honey, they are as irresistible as her savory ravioli.

◇ ◇ ◇

On a clean workspace, mound the flour with a well in the center. Sprinkle the salt evenly over the flour. Add the whole egg and ³/₄ cup warm water into the well and gradually mix into the flour with your hands. When the mixture begins to come together, add the olive oil and knead to fully incorporate. Cover dough with a cloth and let rest at room temperature for 1 hour.

In a mixing bowl, combine the ricotta, sugar, egg yolks, and zests.

On a lightly floured workspace, roll out the dough to a rectangle about ¹/₄ inch thick. Using a sharp paring knife or a large cookie cutter, cut into 3-inch-diameter rounds. Reroll the scraps and cut again as necessary. You should end up with between 24 and 32 rounds.

3¾ cups all-purpose flour
½ teaspoon salt
1 whole egg and 2 egg yolks, divided
½ cup extra virgin olive oil
1½ cups fresh sheep's milk ricotta cheese (or other creamy ricotta cheese, about ¾ pound)
½ cup sugar
Zest of 1 lemon, finely grated
Zest of ½ orange, finely grated
½ cup bitter honey (see page 229)
Vegetable oil for frying
Powdered sugar for dusting

Set aside half of the rounds. With the remaining rounds, lightly mound about 2 tablespoons of the ricotta mixture into the center of each. Top with the other dough rounds and lightly press edges together, crimping edges with a fork to seal. Lightly dust the ravioli with flour to prevent sticking and set aside.

In a saucepan over low heat, warm the bitter honey.

In a deep heavy saucepan, add enough oil to reach a depth of about 2 inches. Place over high heat (oil is ready when a small piece of bread browns in 30 seconds). Fry the ravioli in batches to avoid crowding until golden brown, turning once, approximately 3 to 4 minutes per batch. Remove with a slotted spoon. Set on paper towels to drain. Serve topped with warmed bitter honey and a dusting of powdered sugar.

SA SARTIGLIA

When Carnevale season arrives, nothing compares to the traditions and colorful theatrical spectacle that is Oristano's Sa Sartiglia. More than five centuries old, it takes place on Fat Tuesday and the Sunday before (with a children's festival on Monday), and every guidebook and website makes special note of it. What you see is worth a brief recounting here, too. First, a beautiful procession featuring traditional costumes from all over the island—the women of the town showing off their finery, drummers and trumpeters filling the air with sound, riders on horseback parading past thousands of captivated spectators. Then, Su Cumponidori arrives—the godlike festival king who has been dressed on his throne in an elaborate costume finished with an expressionless ceramic white mask and top hat. He blesses the crowd of thousands with his scepter and opens the ceremony by riding full gallop on his horse.

And now for the spectacle: Su Cumponidori, riding at full speed, aims his scepter and attempts to joust a star-shaped ring suspended by a ribbon high above the ground. Select members from the teams of riders, each in costume and wearing the same expressionless white masks, then do the same with their swords. The more stars successfully pierced, the better the harvest. (The fact that they get any stars at all, given the speed of the ride and size of the star, is astounding but on average one in five succeeds.) The festival then proceeds to the Via Mazzini where the teams of riders perform more seemingly impossible acrobatic rides through the town. (It is as common to see a perfect ride as it is a brutal fall.) For a more intimate look at Sa Sartiglia, see the sidebar on page 179.

Tartlets of sweet cheese and saffron
Casatinas kin Taffaranu

MAKES ABOUT 6 TARTS

The Monday after Easter, Sardinians celebrate the Pasquetta or "Baby Easter." I remember this day as one of the happiest of the year. With winter truly gone, my entire family packed a picnic of roast lamb or suckling pig and headed to the beach. (When I was 15, I killed my first suckling pig for this day.) As we walked to the shore, the lament of the lambs and the bells on the necks of their mothers filled the air. Each of Orosei's hills, covered in blankets of wildflowers, looked like a perfect photograph. When we got there, if the sun was out, it was often warm enough for our first swim. These are the memories I associate with this traditional dessert, which we ate on Easter and at our picnic. Filled with the fresh cheese of spring and the flavor of saffron, every bite, like the day itself, brought a smile.

◇ ◇ ◇

On a clean workspace, mound the flour and stir in baking powder; make a well in the center. Dissolve a pinch of salt in ³/₄ cup warm water. Add 1 of the whole eggs and salted water into the well and gradually mix into the flour with your hands. When mixture begins to come together, add the lard and knead to fully incorporate.

Preheat oven to 350°F.

On a lightly floured workspace, roll out the dough to a ¹/₄-inch thickness. Using a sharp paring knife, cut out 5-inch-diameter rounds. Reroll the scraps together and cut again as needed to yield 6 rounds.

In a medium bowl, stir together the egg yolks, cheeses, sugar, zests, and saffron.

In a small bowl, beat the remaining egg with a splash of water to create an egg wash. Brush the egg wash around the edges of the pasta rounds. Pinch up a ³/₄-inch edge of each pasta round, crimping to create individual shells. The egg wash will help the walls of each shell to stand up straight.

Divide the ricotta mixture among the pasta shells, spreading to fill evenly.

Bake on the center rack for 14 minutes, until top of filling becomes golden.

Cool on a wire rack for about 5 minutes before serving.

3¾ cups all-purpose flour
½ teaspoon baking powder
2 whole eggs and 2 egg yolks, divided
¾ cup lard (or vegetable shortening)
1 cup fresh sheep's milk ricotta cheese (or other creamy ricotta cheese, about ½ pound)
½ cup shredded provolone cheese
½ cup sugar
Zest of 2 oranges, finely grated
Zest of 1 lemon, finely grated
1 pinch saffron

Pane carasau with sweetened ricotta
Pane kin Recottu Durke

At the Sardinian equivalent of a bed and breakfast, bread and ricotta is a common part of the morning meal. But drizzle those ingredients with bitter honey and abbamele and add some berries brightened with a little mint, and you have not only a terrific breakfast but a great dessert. I love the way the abbamele, bitter honey, and cheese combine and balance each other in this treat that requires very little work to make.

◊　◊　◊

In a mixing bowl, gently mix the ricotta, half of the lemon zest, half of the orange zest, and 1 tablespoon of the bitter honey. Mix well, cover, and set aside.

In a sauté pan, combine the lemon and orange juices with the sugar and 1 tablespoon of bitter honey over low heat. Stir until the sugar dissolves. Add the berries and remaining zests and increase heat to medium. Stir and simmer for 4 minutes, reduce heat, and keep warm.

Lightly toast the pane carasau and break each sheet into 4 pieces. Drizzle with the remaining 2 tablespoons of bitter honey.

Stir the chopped mint into the sugared berry mixture. Place the pane carasau pieces on the serving plate and drizzle with the simmered berries. Top with the sweetened ricotta and finish by drizzling the abbamele over all.

1 cup fresh sheep's milk ricotta cheese (or other creamy ricotta cheese
Finely grated zest and juice of 1 lemon
Finely grated zest and juice of 1 orange
4 tablespoons bitter honey (see page 229)
1 tablespoon sugar
1 cup mixed berries
2 whole sheets pane carasau (see page 22)
4 sprigs mint, leaves only, chopped
3 tablespoons abbamele (see page 59)

Almond brittle
Cartò

SERVES 4

I liked helping Zia Zizzi make cartò because she let me eat some when we finished. Not that that stopped me from trying to sneak some while she was still cooking. As she pressed the hot brittle across the table into a large flat sheet, I slipped my fingers up to the edges and grabbed a piece. Of course, my desire to eat was greater than my desire to wait, and I burned my mouth almost every time. Eventually, I learned to hide the piece in a napkin for later. But who could resist Zia Zizzi's cartò? It and Zia Mary's guelfos were always big hits at weddings and baptisms. Some of the cartò was served at the celebration, the rest ended up in the presente de durkes—a basket of treats delivered by the youngest girls as a thank you to close family and friends.

◇　◇　◇

Cut the almonds lengthwise into quarters. Cover a large workspace with parchment paper and sprinkle paper with enough sugar to cover. Line a baking sheet with parchment paper and set aside.

In a large thick-bottomed saucepan (preferably copper), dissolve 1 cup sugar with the honey over medium-low heat. Increase the heat to medium and bring to a boil. Add the almonds and zests. Cook, stirring continuously to prevent sticking with a wooden spoon, until the mixture caramelizes and reaches the soft-ball stage, about 45 minutes. Stir in the liqueur.

Pour the caramel over the sugar on the workspace. Working quickly with an offset spatula, spread out to a rectangular shape of about 1 inch thickness.

When the caramel is set but still warm, cut into long, 1-inch-wide strips with a sharp pastry wheel, and then cut diagonally across into diamonds. Transfer pieces to the baking sheet covered with parchment paper to cool.

2 pounds whole almonds, blanched
1 cup sugar, plus more for work surface
2 cups honey
Zest of 1 orange, finely grated
Zest of 1 lemon, finely grated
1 teaspoon anise liqueur (such as sambuca or anisette)

A LEMON PRESS

Full of almonds and honey with hints of orange and lemon, cartò is worth every bite, but it can be messy to make. Zia Zizzi has one trick to make it a little easier. After pouring the caramelized mixture onto the work surface, she uses a whole lemon to spread and roll it out. The oils in the lemon's skin prevent it from sticking to the hot caramel and it rolls evenly across the top; it also protects her hands from the heat.

Almond balls
Guelfos

MAKES 16 TO 20 CAKES

When it came time for my aunts to make their signature desserts for family celebrations—Zia Zizzi's cartò and Zia Mary's guelfos—they had to share the table during the day. This is no easy trick when you are making treats for hundreds of guests. Close quarters made for a little sisterly competition as they eyed each other's work and offered unsolicited advice. When we were young, my brother Francesco and I raced to find the guelfos when the presente de durkes (basket of treats) was delivered after weddings, greedily unwrapping the paper they came in and gulping them down. Zia Mary's guelfos also appeared at Carnevale celebrations, and I jealously watched her make hundreds of them to share with the town, when I could have easily done away with every one myself.

◊   ◊   ◊

1 pound almonds, whole, blanched
1½ cups sugar, plus more for work surface
Finely grated zest of 1 lemon
1 tablespoon filu'e ferru (see page 170) (or grappa or brandy)

Finely grind the almonds to a powder in a food processor, using quick short bursts to prevent the nuts from becoming oily or pasty.

Cover a large workspace with parchment paper and sprinkle paper with sugar to cover.

In a large thick-bottomed saucepan (preferably copper), heat 2 cups of water over medium-low heat. Add 1½ cups sugar, stirring with a wooden spoon until dissolved. Stir in the zest. Gradually incorporate the almonds while increasing heat to medium. Stir continuously until the mixture reaches a rolling boil, about 10 minutes.

Cook, stirring continuously to prevent sticking, until the soft-ball stage is reached, about 30 to 40 minutes. Test by pulling a small piece from the pan, cooling slightly, and rolling it to see if it stays together. When it reaches the consistency of bread dough, stir in the filu'e ferru. Remove from heat.

Once the almond paste is cool enough to handle safely, moisten the palms of your hands with water to prevent sticking. Taking about a tablespoonful at a time, roll the paste into 1-inch balls.

Place the balls on the sugared parchment paper and roll in sugar. Let cool and wrap individually in wax paper.

PICKING ALMONDS

My brother Francesco and I had the job of helping my father pick the almonds for my aunts' cookies from his orchards. Almonds are everywhere in Sardinia. At the start of spring, their trees create a palette of white and pink flowers across the countryside. Soon the green almonds appear; we pick them off the tree by hand and crack them open to eat the fresh nut inside. By fall, they shed their green skin and turn from white to brown as they dry on the tree. Francesco and I used bamboo sticks to knock them down and gathered them for our family to eat and use in desserts all year long.

Honey pies
Pistiddu

MAKES ABOUT 6 PIES

Sa Esta e san'Antoni e s'Ocu (The Festival of St. Anthony) is one of the most important in Orosei, and indeed all of Sardinia, as it marks the start of Carnevale season (for more, see page 37). St. Anthony is perhaps best known as the patron saint of all four-legged creatures, but he is also the patron saint of bakers. Thus, for this festival in January, Zia Mary took great pride in making this traditional decorative pastry for our family and the town. To make the dozens of pistiddu we brought to the celebration every year, we banded together to help Zia Mary. Over a couple of days, we prepared the filling and the vistire (the "dress")—the top layer cut with intricate designs that finished her beautiful cakes. Finally, as the festival's centerpiece—a fragrant bonfire of rosemary—burned in the church courtyard, we brought the pistiddu into town, sharing them with family, friends, and especially the neediest among us, as well as those just in need of sweet wishes for a healthy and prosperous new year.

◈   ◈   ◈

Prepare the filling: In a large thick-bottomed saucepan (preferably copper), heat the honey and 4 cups water to boiling over medium heat. Stir in the zest. Add the semolina flour, cinnamon, and mosto d'uva; return to a boil. Reduce heat to medium-low and simmer for 30 minutes to thicken, stirring frequently with a wooden spoon to prevent sticking.

Divide the warm mixture evenly among 6 plates. (For best results, use plastic plates about 6 inches wide and 1/2 inch deep for greater flexibility when unmolding the mixture.) Set aside overnight or for at least 8 hours for mixture to cool and set.

2 cups honey
Zest of 1/2 lemon, finely grated
3/4 cup durum semolina flour
1/4 teaspoon cinnamon
1 tablespoon mosto d'uva (see page 42)
3 3/4 cups all-purpose flour
1/2 cup sugar
1 egg yolk
1/2 cup extra virgin olive oil

Prepare the pastry: On a clean workspace, mound the all-purpose flour and stir in the sugar; make a well in the center. Gently beat the egg yolk in a small bowl with 3/4 cup of warm water. Gradually mix the egg and water into the flour with your hands. When mixture begins to come together, add the olive oil and knead to fully incorporate. Cover dough with a cloth and let rest at room temperature for 1 hour.

Preheat oven to 425°F. Line a baking sheet with parchment paper and set aside.

Assemble and cook the dessert: Divide the dough into 6 even pieces. Working with one piece at a time and keeping extra dough covered, roll into a rectangle 7 to 8 inches wide and 14 inches long and about 1/8 inch thick. Cut rectangle in half so you have two twin sheets, each approximately 7 by 7 inches. Gently unmold one of the set honey fillings onto one sheet of the dough.

With a sharp knife or small cookie cutters, cut a decorative pattern out of the other sheet of pastry. Place on top of the filling, so that the filling shows through the pattern's holes. Press gently to let out any air and seal the pastry along the edges. With a crimping pastry wheel, trim around the edges of the filling to create a disk. You should end up with a pastry about 7 inches in diameter.

Repeat with the remaining balls of dough and filling.

Bake the pastries on parchment-lined baking sheets placed on the center rack for 60 to 65 minutes, until the pastry is golden brown and honey filling is bubbly.

PAPASSINOS

When Zia Maria and my sister Angela came to visit me in Texas a few years ago, we found ourselves making another one of the traditional desserts made for Tutti Santi, or All Saints' Day (November 1): papassinos— crisp, diamond-shaped cookies filled with walnuts and raisins. There is not a house in Orosei during Tutti Santi that does not bake them, eat them, or both. I always looked forward to their first appearance in November, when we pay our respects and bring flowers to the graves of relatives who had passed away. These were reflective moments, but they also brought families together as we celebrated their memory. Papassinos are made several times during the year, but if I come home in November, they seem to taste better served with these memories.

Parfait with bitter honey
Semifreddo kin Mele Rankidu
SERVES 4

During the years when the rains made the pastures rich with grass and the cows produced more milk and cream, I remember seeing my family make simple puddings or custards for dessert. Today, those custards have become special desserts, but they still take little more than fresh eggs, cream, and sugar to make. You can find them throughout Sardinia (Zia Maria makes them at her restaurant, Su Barchile), and I love to make them in my restaurants—they are great showcases for abbamele and bitter honey. Today, I prefer the results I get from using gelatin sheets (available in many gourmet stores and supermarkets) to the more common powder.

◇　◇　◇

In a large bowl, whip the heavy cream until soft peaks form.

In a large wide saucepan, add enough water to reach a depth of about 1 inch. Bring to a steady simmer.

In a heavy saucepan that is small enough to fit inside the large saucepan of water, mix the egg yolks and sugar together. Place the saucepan into the simmering water and cook, whisking constantly, over very low heat, until the sugar is dissolved and the mixture is quite warm to the touch, approximately 5 minutes. Be careful not to curdle the eggs by overheating. Remove from heat and let cool to room temperature.

Gently fold the whipped cream into the cooled egg mixture. It's okay if a few streaks remain.

Place the gelatin sheets in a bowl and cover with cold water. Soak for 2 to 3 minutes, until softened. Drain and squeeze any excess water from the sheets. Warm the honey over a very low temperature. Gradually incorporate the softened gelatin into honey, stirring to ensure gelatin is well dissolved.

Carefully stir the honey and gelatin mixture into the cream mixture.

Divide the cream among 8 small ramekins or freezer-proof custard cups. Freeze overnight or for at least 8 hours.

To serve, run a sharp knife around the edges of each ramekin or cup to loosen. Unmold each onto a chilled dessert plate.

Alternatively, you may line a loaf pan with plastic wrap and pour all of the cream into the pan to fill. Once the cream has set, unmold, remove the wrap, and slice.

For yet another special presentation, you may spoon the cream into whole, hollowed-out oranges or lemons whose tops have been cut off. Freeze to set and serve in the shells.

4 cups heavy cream
10 egg yolks
1½ cups sugar
7 sheets gelatin (9 by 2½-inch sheets)
¾ cup bitter honey (see page 229)

Custard with abbamele
Pannacotta kin Abbathu
SERVES 4

Place the gelatin sheets in a bowl and cover with cold water. Soak for 2 to 3 minutes, until softened. Drain and squeeze any excess water from the sheets.

In a large saucepan over medium heat, combine the milk and heavy cream, stirring continuously. Add the softened gelatin, ¼ cup of the abbamele, and sugar. Bring to a gentle boil. Stir the mixture, making sure that the gelatin is well dissolved, and remove from heat.

Pour into small plastic molds or custard cups and cover with plastic wrap. Refrigerate overnight, or at least 8 hours.

Unmold onto individual serving plates. (If pannacotta does not unmold easily, use a knife to loosen the edges and dip the bottoms of the cups into warm water to loosen.) Drizzle each custard with abbamele and top with fresh berries.

3 sheets gelatin (9 by 2½-inch sheets)
1 cup whole milk
2 cups heavy cream
¼ cup abbamele (see page 59), plus more for drizzling
¼ cup sugar
Assorted seasonal berries, for serving

Ricotta fritters
Brungiolos de Carmela

MAKES 12 TO 16 PASTRIES

When I have time for a meal in Berchidda (my Sardinian home away from home, see page 109), Carmela, my friend Pasquale's mother, makes these delicious ricotta pastries for us. Brungiolos are a specialty of the Gallura region, and her recipe is my favorite; the sweetness comes only from the creamy ricotta, while a touch of parsley gives them a pleasing herbal quality. Although she makes only a small batch for us, Carmela fries hundreds of them for celebrations, especially weddings, which in Sardinia require a week or more of preparation just for the food.

◊　◊　◊

Place the ricotta in a fine-mesh sieve and let sit over a bowl in the refrigerator for at least an hour to drain.

Dissolve the yeast in ¹/₄ cup of warm water. Let sit for 2 to 3 minutes, until the mixture foams.

In a medium bowl, combine the drained ricotta with the egg. Add the salt, parsley, yeast mixture, and the ¹/₂ cup of flour. Mix well.

In a deep heavy saucepan, add enough oil to reach a depth of about 5 inches. Place over high heat (oil is ready when a small piece of bread browns in 30 seconds).

With your hands, form the ricotta mixture into 2-inch balls and lightly roll in flour to coat. Fry in small batches, turning once, until golden brown, 2 to 3 minutes. Remove with a slotted spoon. Place on paper towels to drain and cool.

Warm the bitter honey in a small saucepan over low heat.

Serve the brungiolos while still warm, drizzled with honey and dusted with sugar.

2 cups fresh sheep's milk ricotta cheese (or other creamy ricotta cheese)

1 teaspoon active dry yeast

1 egg

¹/₄ teaspoon salt

1 teaspoon finely chopped flat leaf parsley

¹/₂ cup all-purpose flour, plus more for coating

Vegetable oil for frying

Bitter honey (see page 229) for drizzling

Powdered sugar for dusting

WEDDINGS

Carmela needs hundreds of brungiolos (see page 249) for weddings in Berchidda, because when someone from Berchidda gets married, the whole town comes. This is not so strange when you consider that more than 80 percent of Sardinians are related to the original settlers of the town in which they live. The town isn't *like* a family; it *is* family. In the rest of Sardinia, the most traditional weddings are like family reunions with 400 people or more crowding the town like a festival. Families plan for months and take a week or more to set up—from making up the home for the bride and groom (see page 253) to preparing meats like suckling pig (see page 166) and desserts like cartò and guelfos, as well as covering a huge area with a tent for the celebration. For me, as a boy, helping everyone get ready was so much fun it felt like vacation. After the wedding, we had lunch and performed traditional dances through the afternoon until dinner—then we danced and laughed and sang into the night. Coming back home, exhaustion mixed with pride and relief that the whole celebration was over. And I knew there would be some new sweets in our pantry for days to come.

Winter apple confection
Kintonzatu

SERVES 4

When I first saw winter apples in Mannai Carta's dresser drawers or lining her closets, I thought they were treasure boxes. Then, one day she told me she used them to make those places smell good, like potpourri, and also to make this special candy. Looking at them, I could not understand why anyone would eat them. They don't look like "normal" apples; they are hairy and very hard and tart, even when they ripen in December and January. But then my grandmother cooked the apples to soften them and release their juices and mixed them with almonds and honey to make this sweet treat; I would never again doubt that something so good could come from something so ugly.

◇   ◇   ◇

Preheat oven to 350°F.

On a baking sheet, toast the almonds until golden brown and set aside to cool.

Cover a large workspace with parchment paper and cover paper with sugar.

Wash the apples well, then bake for 1 hour on a baking sheet. Let cool slightly, quarter, and core, leaving skin on. Puree the quartered apples in a food processor. You should have about 3 cups of apple puree.

In a large thick-bottomed saucepan (preferably copper) over medium-high heat, bring honey to a boil until it begins to foam on the top. Fold in the apple puree and reduce heat to medium. Cook, stirring frequently to prevent sticking, for 30 to 35 minutes or until the mixture comes together. When the mixture reaches the consistency of bread dough, stir in the ½ cup sugar and almonds and continue cooking for 5 minutes longer, stirring often.

Pour the apple mixture over sugar-covered parchment. With an offset spatula, spread the mixture out to a 1½-inch thickness. You must work quickly before the candy hardens.

When the candy is set but still warm, cut into long, 1-inch-wide strips with a sharp pastry wheel, and then cut diagonally across into diamonds. Transfer pieces to a baking sheet covered with parchment paper to cool.

Store wrapped in wax paper in a cool, dry place.

1 cup slivered almonds

2 pounds winter apples (or crabapples)

3 cups honey

½ cup sugar, plus more for work surface

Candied orange peel
Aranzata
SERVES 4

Mannai Carta knew that the best way to attract children, keep them close, and show them her love was to offer food. The value of food in my family was and remains very high. Giving food to someone else is like giving a part of you. In winter, when the oranges were in season, my grandmother sat by the fireplace and offered me one. I sat beside her and watched as she carefully peeled it so the rind would not break. She then handed me the orange and hung the rind to dry by the fire to use in making saba, to flavor desserts, or to make this sweet candy that would surely draw me back to her side, just as my mother does with my children today.

◇ ◇ ◇

Using a sharp paring knife, cut the rind away from the oranges. It is fine, even preferable, if some of the bitter white pith remains attached to the rind. Slice the rind into ¼-inch-wide strips. You should end up with about 2 cups.

4 to 6 medium oranges (preferably a thick-skinned variety)
¼ cup thinly sliced almonds
1½ cups honey
Sugar

Place the rind in a bowl and cover with water. Let sit covered, at room temperature, overnight, or at least 8 hours.

Drain the rind and set aside. In a large pot, bring 4 cups fresh water to a boil. Blanch the soaked rind for 5 minutes. Drain, wrap in a clean kitchen towel, and wring to remove excess water.

Preheat oven to 350°F. On a baking sheet, toast the almonds until golden brown and set aside to cool. Line a sheet pan with parchment paper and cover paper with sugar.

In a large thick-bottomed saucepan (preferably copper) over medium-high heat, bring honey to a boil until it begins to foam on the top. Fold in orange rind and reduce heat to medium. Cook, stirring frequently to avoid sticking, for 30 to 35 minutes or until mixture reaches the consistency of bread dough. Stir in the toasted almonds and cook for 5 minutes longer.

Drop heaping tablespoonfuls of the candy mixture onto the sugared sheet pan and let cool. Serve in small paper liners (such as cupcake liners) or as is. Store wrapped in wax paper in a cool, dry place.

HOME IS WHERE THE HEARTH IS

Mannai Carta's fireplace was in her house, and her house was our first home. It was traditional in Sardinia for a son to move back home with his wife until he could afford to build his own home—and this is what my parents did, too. A room or section of the house was set aside for the newlyweds and in the days before the wedding, the family would begin gathering all the things the couple needed—from linens to pots and pans—to set up their "house." Friends, family, and honored guests would then bring the wedding presents, which were put on display so all could see what each person had given. In the years to come, as the young couple started their family and worked and saved for their future, the grandparents became their "trainers" in marriage and life—as Mannai Carta and Mannoi Arre were for my parents.

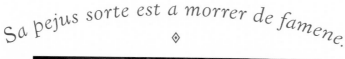

Sa pejus sorte est a morrer de famene.

◇

"Hunger is the worst of all fates."

AFTERWORD

Over Here

Alfonso Silba was my junior high school art professor, but when I visit him today in his Orosei studio, I think of him as my professor in life. His striking, modern murals cover the walls of my restaurants and office in the United States, reminding me every day of his tireless effort to capture the stories and history of our island and keep them alive for generations to come. That is what I wanted to do in this book: to capture through these recipes not just the food but the people, stories, traditions, and history behind them and preserve them for the future.

It took me more than twenty years to realize this dream. I have spent my first two decades in the United States introducing American palates to the flavors of Sardinia and sharing my love for the island in almost everything I make and do—even the granite and marble for the bars, tables, and floors at my restaurants come from the mountains of Orosei and quarries where my father worked. The name gracing both my restaurants, Arcodoro (arch of gold in Italian), reflects my love: it is the name of the arch of the church in Orosei where the bonfire starting the festival of St. Anthony is held every year. When I was away and thought of the place I loved, this arch was what I saw in my mind. And now I know others will see it, too.

This book is my love letter—my inheritance and my legacy.

Salute!

Planning a Trip to Sardinia

As awareness of Sardinia's unique culture and cuisine increases, I am happy to see the tourism industry surge throughout the island, not just in the Porto Cervo area. My wife and I are often asked for tips and recommendations for must-see stops on a trip to the island. I mention throughout the book many places and sites that are not only important parts of my childhood but wonderful places to visit to truly experience Sardinia. But here are some specific addresses you might find useful in planning a trip.

When it comes to lodging, throughout Sardinia you will find many establishments that fall somewhere between a full-service hotel and what in the United States we would call a bed and breakfast. These are smaller, often family-operated, hotels which offer a full range of meals, services, and hospitality. They serve as your home away from home. Of course it is important to always call in advance to make reservations and confirm which services are provided. For more current travel information, also check out the websites mentioned in For Further Reading on page 261.

Hotels

Club Hotel Torre Moresca
Loc Cala Ginepro
Orosei (OT)
Tel: 0784-91230
www.torremoresca.it

Colonna Pevero Beach Hotel
Loc. Golfo del Pevero
Porto Cervo (OT)
Tel: 0789-25852

Hotel Gallura
C. Umberto 145
Olbia (OT)
Tel: 0789-24648

Hotel Maria Rosaria
Via Grazia Deledda 13
Orosei (NU)
Tel: 0784-98657

Hotel Mediterraneo
Via Montello 3
Olbia (OT)
Tel: 0879-24173

Hotel Ristorante Su Barchile
Via Mannu 5
Orosei (NU)
Tel: 0784-98879
www.subarchile.it

Hotel San Marco
Piazzetta San Marco
Porto Rotondo (OT)
Tel: 0789-34110

Restaurants

Agriturismo Testone
Loc Sa Serra (countryside)
Nuoro (NU)
Tel: 0784-98879
www.agriturismotestone.com

La Ghinghetta
Via Cavour 26
Portoscuso (CA)
Tel: 0781-508143

Ristorante da Achille
Via Nazionale 82
Sant'Antioco (CA)
Tel: 0781-83105
www.albergoristorantemoderno.
  com

Ristorante da Adri's
Via d'Annunzio
Olbia (OT)
Tel: 0789-21118
www.daadris.com

Ristorante da Nicolo
Via G. Bruno
Carloforte (CA)
Tel: 0781-857101
www.danicolo.com

Ristorante da Renzo
Km. 99 Siamaggiore
Oristano (OT)
Tel: 0783-33658
www.darenzo.it

Ristorante Grazia Deledda
Strada per Baia Sardinia
Arzachena (OT)
Tel: 0789-98990

Ristorante Il Senato
Via Gioacchino Mundula
Sassari (SS)
Tel: 079-231423

Ristorante I Quattroventi
Loc. Monte Petrosu
San Teodoro (OT)
Tel: 0784-835241

Ristorante La Mola
Loc. Piccolo Pevero
Porto Cervo (OT)
Tel: 0789-92313

Ristorante Sa Cardiga e Su Schironi
Loc. Maddalena Spiaggia
Capoterra (CA)
Tel: 070-71652

Ristorante Su Gologone
Loc. Su Gologone
Oliena (NU)
Tel: 0784-287512
http://www.sugologone.it

The Sardinian Pantry

Sardinian products used to be impossible to find in the states, even for a restaurateur. But today many are available at gourmet local food stores and even larger specialty food chains. All of the Sardinian indigenous ingredients mentioned in the book are available online through my own company, GourmetSardinia, as well as through other online gourmet shops:

ChefShop.com (www.chefshop.com) offers some of Sardinia's harder-to-find ingredients, tel: 1-800-596-0885.

GourmetSardinia (www.gourmetsardinia.com) for ordering and information on the Sardinian products we import ourselves.

Igourmet.com (www.Igourmet.com) offers a variety of Sardinian cheeses and other products, tel: 1-877-IGOURMET.

Olio 2 Go (www.olio2go.com) for fine Italian olive oils.

The Chefs Warehouse (www.chefswarehouse.com) assorted gourmet products from around the world.

Zingerman's (www.zingermans.com) for an array of Italian cheeses, pastas, and other unique ingredients.

For Further Reading

Sardinia really is, as people say, an island of experiences. I hope you will go there to create your own. All of the stories and most of the information in this book come from me, my family, and the people I know and work with in Sardinia. When I needed information or clarification, I turned to them first and foremost. To check on my Sardo, I consulted my friend Giovanni Maria Cabras and his terrific Sardo-Italian dictionary *Vocabolariu Baroniesu* (Torino: Trauben, 2003).

Unfortunately, there is not a tremendous amount of literature about Sardinia or by Sardinians in English. This cookbook cited only two: D. H. Lawrence's *Sea and Sardinia* (New York: Penguin, 1921, revised edition 1999) and Grazia Deledda's *Reeds in the Wind* (New York: Italica Press, 1999).

To check on a fact or specific information, Jim and I mostly turned to travel guides. The authors are not all Sardinian but they spent months researching and re-visiting the island. Sardinia's growing popularity as a tourist attraction has led to dozens of new and recently revised editions of these guides: *Cadogan's Sardinia* (Guilford, CT: Cadogan Guides, 2007), *The Rough Guide to Sardinia* (New York: Rough Guides, 2007), *The Lonely Planet Guide to Sardinia* (Oakland, CA: Lonely Planet Publications, 2006), and *Authentic Sardinia* by the Touring Club of Italy (Dover, NH: Touring Club of Italy, 2006). Also useful is *Wine Routes in Sardinia* by the D.O.C. Wine Consortium (Consorzio Vini D.O.C. di Sardegna, 1999) for background on wine in Sardinia.

Less reliable but quite bountiful is the Internet. Every day, we found more Web pages and blogs on Sardinia and Sardinian food. Few are Sardinian or run by Sardinians but they are often passionate about the island and its cuisine. The biggest sites contain good and up-to-date information on the cities and events, such as www.sardinia.net, www.sardegna.com, and www.sardegnaedintorni.com with its companion periodical publication *Sardegna e Dintorni*.

I have many English-language cookbooks, and these days you might find one of our indigenous Sardinian ingredients or a recipe for one of our dishes in books by Mario Batali (who made pane frattau with me and my brother Francesco) and Susan Hermann Loomis (who went with me to Sardinia) and many more. And of course, we acknowledge Giuliano Bugialli's *Foods of Sicily and Sardinia and the Smaller Islands* (New York: Rizzoli, 1996) as the only American cookbook that mentions Sardinia in its title (about a third of the recipes are Sardinian in origin). We consulted some of these books as well as a few reference books not written in English, especially: *Pane, Tradizione e prospettive della panificazione in Sardegna* compiled by Anna Pau (Nuoro: Illisso Edizioni 2005), a compilation of articles by various authors on Sardinian bread from all over the island with great information on the differences in breads from region to region, and

Pastoritudine, Atto II by Annico Pau (Cagliari: Edinsar, 1994), a history of the Sardinian shepherd and the shepherd culture.

Finally, there are an ever-growing number of articles in food magazines like *Food & Wine, Saveur,* and *The Magazine of La Cucina Italiana.* We always check them to see who is writing about what, but the recipes in the book are from my family and me (as are some in those magazines–most notably *La Cucina Italiana,* which has featured many of our recipes, and the May 2005 issue of *Food & Wine,* which featured a version of our Perdinzanu Prenu). The article mentioned on page 128 of this book is "The Secrets of Long Life" by Dan Buettner (*National Geographic,* November 2005). The article mentioned on page 131 is "Oenology: Red wine procyanidins and vascular health" by Professor Roger Corder (*Nature,* November 30, 2006).

Acknowledgments

The soul of this book is Sardinia but its heart is my family, and my thanks start from those closest to my heart. First, my wife, Lori, who is everything to me: spouse, partner, friend, and confidant. She shares my dreams, indulges every crazy idea, honors my passions, and returns my love. She has also given me two beautiful children, Valerio and Francesca. Valerio shares my passion at the table and does not consider it a meal unless there is a napkin, knife, and fork. Francesca shares my love of the kitchen and the garden and has been my favorite sous-chef her whole life. They make me proud every day. Thank you to Lori's parents, Carl and Patricia, who have given us so much. And to my parents, Giuliano and Caterina; my brothers, Salvatore and Francesco; my sisters, Angela and Teresa; and the rest of my family whom you've met throughout the book, both living and gone: Thank you for your stories, recipes, inspiration, guidance, frequent phone consults, love, and support as I wrote this book.

This book would not be possible without the friendship and help of my greater Sardinian "family"–the people who preserve Sardinian traditions and those whose friendship inspire me: Pasquale Rau and his family in Berchidda for years of friendship and our common mission to share the wonders of Sardinian gastronomy; Gianni and Rosanna Scanu for opening their home and the wonderful evenings in the cucina rustica; Massimo Apeddu for welcoming us to his country home and sharing his passion for our island; Giansanto Calvia for his wonderful ricotta and sharing his artisanal cheese factory in Berchidda with us; Gesuino Galaffu and Sergio Crasta (Giogantinu) for opening their cantina to us to taste their wonderful wines and share their passion for Sardinian grapes; Pietro and Donatella Medde for the fine demonstration and discussion of making fregula; Cesello and Alessio Putzu for showing us their family's rice factory and their commitment to quality Sardinian rice production; Mattiu Spina and his lovely family for preserving the traditions of Sardinian goat shepherding and his finely crafted spits; Diego Feurra for the tour of Seneghe and sharing the legacy of the Red Cow; Giorgio Pala for his passion for Sa Sartiglia and taking us "inside" this beautiful tradition; Emilio Piras for his commitment to the preservation of bottarga; Domenico Pira and his family for showing us the beauty of traditional cheesemaking; Andrea Loriga and his brothers for their quality olive oil production; Giovanni Maria Cabras for his preservation of and guidance through the Sardo language; my friend Giulio Rondoni, who happens to be my brother-in-law; Antonio Mele and Antonello Loi for their partnership and support; Gavino Cambosu for our lifelong friendship and support; Alfonso Silba for a lifetime of friendship and inspiration; and lastly my mentor, Tonino Corbeddu, and his wife, Marisa, for everything they have done and continue to do for me.

When I was deep in the book, both here and in Sardinia, my extended family in Texas kept our company and restaurants going every day: Giancarlo Ferrara, who helped prepare the recipes for testing and whose cooking in the Houston restaurant inspires me daily; my brother Francesco in the Dallas restaurant, whose garden full of myrtle takes me home; and everyone else who keeps Arcodoro and Arcodoro & Pomodoro humming. This includes my management team of Christiano Conte, Sergio Oregon, Joe Ramos, Abby Dudziak, Luigi Shimaj, and Suzette Roberts as well as the greatest staff anyone has had the pleasure of working with (some of whom have been with me since the beginning). To the hundreds of loyal customers who have embraced Sardinia and me for all these years: thank you for joining us at the table. I must also mention the staff of the GourmetSardinia office who work tirelessly to get my authentic Sardinian products into the kitchens of America. And in that office, no one shared the passion and determination for this book more than Amy Nielsen, who has been by my side for ten years and saw through completion the first recipes and the last and cheered every new ingredient along the way. She was the liaison between Jim and myself, and we appreciate all she did.

The book family begins with our editor, Christopher Steighner at Rizzoli, who recognized the potential for the book from his first email, guided us coolly through its creation, and most of all, came up with the title we all love. Thank you to my agent Lisa Ekus for believing in my vision and my quest and leading us to Chris. Thanks also to others at Rizzoli: publisher Charles Miers, Jonathan Jarrett in editorial, and Pam Sommers in publicity. Also let's recognize our extended book family: the extraordinary and insightful copy editor Anne O'Connor, the proofreader Lynn Scrabis, the recipe tester Paige Boyle, and the designer Laura Lindgren for her beautiful pages. Those pages needed inspired design to match the food photography of Laurie Smith (and her assistant Annie Slocum and stylist Erica McNeish) and the pictures from Sardinia by Rohan Van Twest, who is not only a brilliant photographer but on every trip we take a never-dull, sharp-witted traveling companion. Finally, thanks to Jim Eber for your friendship and support, but most of all for your words. You took my life and crafted it into this wonderful tribute to my family and the island that I love.

And from Jim: Thank you, Efisio, for believing in me as your writing partner and turning me into your "Sardinian Monster." You and Lori have always made me feel like family in our decade (and counting) of friendship. Salute! Thank you to Janet and Jerry Eber, Adele Richter, Thea Trachtenberg, and Heidi Krupp for all you did in helping me get the words out. And to my wife, Amy, whom I could not love more: Your careful reads, thoughtfulness, enthusiasm, pride, and love touch me and this book and inspire the youngest of the Sardinian Monsters, our son, Simon, who cannot wait to sit at the table with Francesca, Valerio, and the rest of his Texan and Sardinian family.

Conversion Chart

All conversions are approximate.

LIQUID CONVERSIONS	
U.S.	Metric
1 tsp	5 ml
1 tbs	15 ml
2 tbs	30 ml
3 tbs	45 ml
¼ cup	60 ml
⅓ cup	75 ml
½ cup	120 ml
⅔ cup	150 ml
¾ cup	180 ml
1 cup	240 ml
1¼ cups	300 ml
1⅓ cups	325 ml
1½ cups	350 ml
1⅔ cups	375 ml
1¾ cups	400 ml
2 cups (1 pint)	475 ml
2½ cups	600 ml
3 cups	720 ml
4 cups (1 quart)	945 ml (1,000 ml is 1 liter)

WEIGHT CONVERSIONS	
U.S./U.K.	Metric
½ oz	14 g
1 oz	28 g
1½ oz	43 g
2 oz	57 g
2½ oz	71 g
3 oz	85 g
3½ oz	100 g
4 oz	113 g
5 oz	142 g
6 oz	170 g
7 oz	200 g
8 oz	227 g
9 oz	255 g
10 oz	284 g
11 oz	312 g
12 oz	340 g
13 oz	368 g
14 oz	400 g
15 oz	425 g
1 lb	454 g

OVEN TEMPERATURES		
°F	Gas Mark	°C
250	½	120
275	1	140
300	2	150
325	3	165
350	4	180
375	5	190
400	6	200
425	7	220
450	8	230
475	9	240
500	10	260
550	Broil	290

Index

641.59459 FAR
Farris, Efisio.
Sweet myrtle & bitter honey

1-7-08

Watchung Public Library
12 Stirling Road
Watchung, NJ 07069

FRANCE

VENICE

GENOA

MONACO
NICE   LIVORNO   FLORENCE

MARSEILLE

LIGURIAN SEA

ADRIATIC SEA

ITALY

SPAIN

Corsica   *Elba*

AJACCIO

ROME

BARCELONA

BALEARIC ISLANDS

SARDINIA

Minorca

NAPLES

Majorca

TYRRHENIAN SEA

Ibiza

CAGLIARI

PALERMO

MEDITERRANEAN SEA

SICILY

ALGIERS

ALGERIA

TUNIS

VALLET

MALTA

TUNISIA